ADVANCE PRAISES

When Love Wags a Tail is a delightful collection of feel-good tales about remarkable canine encounters that prove that dogs really are our best friends.

—Kerk Murray, International bestselling author of *Pawprints on Our Hearts*

The therapeutic value of a trauma survivor's relationship with their dog is something I routinely see in my practice as a licensed professional therapist. *When Love Wags a Tail* is an unforgettable, beautifully written gift to dog lovers everywhere.

—Angela Miller, Licensed Professional Therapist

With irrepressible spirit, humor, and charm, Leal seamlessly weaves in stories about the meaning of various flowers and shrubs in her yard and shares the parallels between man's best friend and plants.

— Brian Pribbernow, Gardener, dog lover, professional florist and owner of uBloom, a creative boutique and gift store

You will alternately smile, shed tears, laugh out loud, and be warmed by the stories within these pages as you read how love literally "wags its tail" and enters your life and your heart.

— Carol Vogel, Retired college professor and dog lover

Through the lens of these diverse narratives, *When Love Wags a Tail* showcases how these remarkable creatures often become the saviors of souls in need of solace. I wholeheartedly recommend this book to anyone who has ever experienced the indescribable joy of loving a dog.

—Stefan Dubiel, Host of ThoughtVolution, a podcast that captures the essence of lived experiences

When Love Wags a Tail

Inspiring Stories of Love, Loyalty, and Laughter

CARMEN LEAL

WAG AWAY
PUBLISHING

in coordination with EA Books Publishing, a division of Living Parables

When Love Wags a Tail, Inspiring Stories of Love, Loyalty, and Laughter
By Carmen Leal
Copyright © 2024

ISBN: 978-1-963611-09-0
LCCN: 2024905031

Cover photo: Dog photo by Aaron Jankowski/a.pet.ure; BlackeyedSusans, iStock/Kyle Robinson
Author photo courtesy of Aaron Jankowski/a.pet.ure
Cover design by Robin Black

Wag Away Publishing, LLC
Oshkosh, WI
Wagawaypublishing.com

in partnership with
EA Books Publishing, a division of
Living Parables of Central Florida, Inc. a 501c3
EABooksPublishing.com

TABLE OF CONTENTS

Dedication . . . . **ix**

Foreword:

    A Piece of the Puzzle by Cheryl Hentz 1

Opening the Garden Gate: Goldenrod **5**

    It Really Is a Dog Book 6

Chapter One: Daffodil **9**

    Positive Changes 10

    A Surprising Souvenir by Andrea Hunter 13

    A New Life with Baby by Tricia Stertz as told by Herb Doemel . . 16

    The Cool Mom 19

    A Tornado on Four Paws by Kristine Lowder 23

    Dawdle and Sniff 26

    Charlie's Song by Michele Miles Gardiner 29

    Tears for Natalie by Janice Thompson. 33

Chapter Two: Black-Eyed Susan **36**

    Matt's Memory Garden 37

    Polly the Grunting Pig Dog 40

    Growing Old with Dior by Elizabeth Ritzman. 43

    Our First Rescue Plants 47

    Our "Purebred Pooch" by Charlotte H. Burkholder. 50

    Lightbulb Moments by Edwina Ditmore 54

    Spoiled in All the Best Ways by Sandra Dennis 58

Chapter Three: Milkweed **61**

    Grandpa's Not Just Eight 62

    Hope Isn't Always Noisy by Don Hughes. 65

    Filling an Empty Nest by Leola R. Ogle 69

    Love Like Blackberries by Brenda Kay Ledford 73

    The Happiest Ending Ever by Karlene Leatherman. 76

    The Heart Stealer by Carla Stewart 79

    The Joy of Being Merry by Gail Westrup 83

Chapter Four: Sunflower **87**

Sunflower Dogs 88

A Tricolor Ball of Energy by Debra Mahoney. 90

Dogs of BrooksHaven by Peggy Frezon 93

It Started with Misty by Susan E. Mullaney 96

Our Perfect Foster Fail by Margot Bennett 99

Stubborn in a Good Way by Rosie Maureen 103

Unexpected Heroes by Diane Huff Pitts 107

Made to Serve by Xochitl Dixon 110

Chapter Five: Hydrangea. **116**

Girl on the Run. 117

A Star Named Lucy by Chris Trollinger 121

Brandy, the Licking Machine by Sally Apokedak 125

God Spelled Backward by Quentin Wood 128

Formerly Known as Stubby Tail by Denise Mullard 134

Marley the Pub Dog by Eileen Joyce Donovan 138

Meant to be Murdock by Gerald Hendrickson. 141

Chapter Six: Bird of Paradise **144**

The Courage to Grow. 145

A Chance to Love by Diane Smits 147

And Then I Got a Dog 151

A Therapy Dog Washout by Janet Charbonneau 154

The Skinny Dog I Never Knew I Needed by Stevie Anderson . . . 157

My Repurposed Life. 160

One Day at a Time by Rosie Maureen as told by
Joyce Bean Leeman 164

Broken Isn't Useless. 167

Hobie's Half-Way House by Ellie Ray Spivey 170

Chapter Seven: New England Aster **173**

Unwavering Love. 174

Baby Halle's Legacy by Janet Pfeiffer. 177

Doing the Impossible 180

Molly's Marvelous Family by Carolyn Fisher. 184

Miko and Me by Zeta Davidson as told to by Charles Dakin 188

Coconut Farts 191

The Changing of the Guard by Anne Foley Rauth. 193

Teddy Knew by Mary J. Hahn 196

Chapter Eight: Phlox **199**

My Most Compatible Companion 200

Karlie's Lessons by Andie LaComb 203

Not "Just a Dog" by Roxanne Rolph 207

The Perfect Sleep Aid. 209

The Best of Them All by Margaret (Peg) Olson 212

The Gift that Rescued Us All by Pat Severin. 215

Life after Goodbye by Melinda Schmidt 218

What Do You See? By Marsha Hubler 221

Latching the Garden Gate: Hostas: **223**

Welcome Home 224

One Dog at a Time by Sandra Dennis 227

Find a Need 230

Paying Homage to Our Dogs by Cheryl Hentz 233

Contributors **235**

Acknowledgements **243**

Photo Credits. **244**

Dear Reader. **245**

To the members of the Wisconsin Gardening Facebook Group. Thank you for the warm welcome, for answering every dumb question, for cheering me on when something went right, and for those of you who gave me rescue plants.

Also dedicated to The Ladies Who Brunch. Thank you for the laughter, the calories, and the holiday drinks.

A PIECE OF THE PUZZLE
Cheryl Hentz

"We can judge the heart of a man by his treatment to animals."
— Immanuel Kant

When I was a child, we were never without a dog. In fact, we always had more than one, and my brother and I learned as young children to love and respect them; to treat them right; and to always care for them.

Family takes care of family, and that includes our dogs. Both my brother and I have carried this philosophy forward with the many canines we've had as adults. Like a cherished memento that keeps getting handed down from one generation to another, so does our love for our furry friends.

As a young adult, I found myself wanting to do more for animals, especially dogs, since they were, and remain, the animals I knew best. I began volunteering with local animal shelters by writing/editing their newsletters and serving on the board of directors for the Oshkosh Area Humane Society in Oshkosh, Wisconsin.

I was honored to do both, but was especially thrilled as a board member to be part of a successful capital campaign allowing our local shelter to move from an over-crowded, depressing, archaic building, to a modern, spacious, and animal-friendly location.

As I began to understand the process and how rescue groups work to get these dogs adopted, I knew I needed to take on more of an advocacy role. My dogs have always been adopted from shelters or rescue groups so it made sense to use my talents in those arenas.

I started with an organization that rehomed Dalmatians and Dalmatian mixes. This opened my eyes to the bigger need, and I started volunteering with other rescue groups, doing all kinds of tasks. When most people consider the needs at a shelter, they think of socializing dogs or taking them for walks or other hands-on activities. I was comfortable in those roles, but I realized that I had been developing skills my entire life that others didn't have; skills that I could put to good use helping animals in shelters and rescues, and by volunteering with other animal welfare and advocacy groups.

As a writer, working on newsletters was certainly something I could do. But I was soon doing other much-needed tasks: doing home visits for those interested in adoption, making follow-up calls to people who'd adopted a month or even several months earlier, and transporting dogs from one location to another.

I also was doing several different activities for the Humane Society of the United States including setting up a table at different local or area events. I and other volunteers tried to get more people signed up to help the HSUS with other necessary tasks, such as writing letters to the editor about animal-related issues in the news, lobbying elected officials about pending legislative issues, etc. At the end of the day, there's strength in numbers and you can get more done when there's thousands of people with the same mindset as opposed to hundreds or dozens.

I also learned that the HSUS had a faith ministries program and I helped start and facilitate an animal ministries program at my church. The HSUS has since done away with the faith ministries program, but my own church group will soon be entering its 11th year.

Through this group and some of my other efforts, I met Carmen Leal. We became friends over the years, and she asked me to write this foreword because the need for volunteers is so critical to the survival of not just animals, but also the organizations that work so tirelessly to save them.

One cautionary word, however. Just as employees at animal organizations (or any nonprofit, really) can suffer from work-related burnout, volunteers can also experience something called volunteer burnout or compassion and empathy fatigue. The only difference is volunteers don't get paid to power through it.

Periodically, I feel compassion fatigue. I get frustrated with things. No matter how much work we do, so much more always has to be done. There are also rare occasions when I feel like I may not be making a difference. This is especially true when I see the people from the Humane Society of the United States, the ASPCA, or other similar groups, going into hoarding or cruelty situations, or when natural disasters have occurred, to rescue multiple animals. It's easy to feel that unless you're a "boots on the ground" person, you're not making a difference.

During those few times when I feel this way, I focus on what I know to be true, and it's a saying I first became familiar with decades ago: "Saving one animal won't change the world, but it will surely change the world for that one animal." There are slight variations of this statement, and it's been attributed to different people over the years, but it's just as true today as it was when it was originally penned by whoever first wrote it.

There's no question that you'll be emotionally moved by this book so keep a tissue handy. But I hope it will also move you to volunteer in some way for animals. There is always work to be done, and there is always a need for people to do that work, especially as longtime volunteers age out or pass on. No matter what your talent, skills, or level of interest and ability, giving of yourself, even in a small way, makes a big difference in the grand scheme of things. Like me, you probably have knowledge or skills that are important and can help save lives.

Saving animals requires people doing all kinds of jobs, including those things I do. Each role we play is a piece of the puzzle and, without each piece, the puzzle cannot be completed. The nice thing about there being all kinds of jobs within rescue, shelter, or animal advocacy and welfare work is that no matter how old we are or may get to be, and as our physical abilities change with age, every person can still do something.

We will always need people to adopt dogs and to give them wonderful, loving, "fur"-ever homes. You'll read about many of them in this book. Maybe you're among those people who have adopted from a shelter or rescue. Kudos to you for doing that. But I would encourage you to search your soul and think about how you might be able to help a dog, cat, or other animal besides adopting it. There's not a shelter, rescue, or animal group around that ever has enough funding or supplies. And while money and supplies are appreciated, what else can you do?

Maybe you have space for one more dog that needs to be fostered. Skills such as accounting, marketing, letter-writing, fundraising, making phone calls, handing out materials, and doing transportation are all needed in any animal organization, and these are just the beginning of the many jobs you and others can do. Whether you want to be a "boots on the ground" person in the thick of things and often at the center of attention in a hoarding or abuse situation, or you want to work behind the scenes in practical obscurity, you are needed, and will always be appreciated for the difference you are making.

When you use your unique talents and life experiences to help animals you will not only feel good, but you'll be saving lives. Please, think about an animal rescue, shelter, or welfare/advocacy organization or two closest to your heart, and inquire of them how you can help. You'll never feel as good as you will by donating your time and talent to help the animals who can't help themselves and by being a voice for animals who can't speak for themselves.

As you read this book, I would encourage you to think about how you can help. If every person volunteered just one or two hours a week—even a month, think about the difference we could make not only in our own community, but in the country and the world! Please step up and help, won't you?

OPENING THE GARDEN GATE
GOLDENROD POSITIVITY

"Stories have power. They delight, enchant, touch, teach, recall, inspire, motivate, challenge. They help us understand."

– Janet Litherland

IT REALLY IS A DOG BOOK

When I was at a signing last year, a man I had never met stood in line with a copy for me to autograph. He was just an average, middled-aged guy—one I probably would not recognize on the street if I walked past him again. I've since had others bring books they have bought online or received as gifts, but he was the first one I encountered during the eleven events I did in the first two months after the release of *I Chose You.*

As he handed me his copy, he muttered that he didn't really like dogs. I assured him that I had not been a big fan of man's best friend before I had adopted Coconut. I thought he had purchased it as a gift for his wife or mother, so I was surprised when he asked me to add his name when I personalized his copy.

I frequently post on several local social media sites on a variety of topics, so it wasn't surprising that he knew who I was since he'd seen the article about me in the local newspaper. As I was writing a message and my name, he explained that since he had wanted to support a local author, he ordered a copy from Amazon.

I had barely said thank you when he responded, with more than a little outrage, that this wasn't a book about dogs. The subtitle alone should have told him it was a dog book. And then there was the cover with a photo of a dog kissing a woman. Or it might have been the other way around. Either way, a dog was on the cover.

"This isn't a book about dogs," he repeated. "This is a book about you!"

There are a lot of stories about me inside those pages, and I'll be the first to admit that not every one of them has anything to do with dogs. But it's mostly about dogs. A lot of dogs. In fact, stories from forty-four other dog owners are included in the book. So, yeah, it's a dog book.

I handed him back his copy and thanked him for supporting me and other local authors. He turned to walk away, stopped, looked over his shoulder, and with a big grin said, "And this book don't even suck!"

The people in line laughed and my fan sauntered off, looking quite proud of himself.

That has to be one of the weirdest and best compliments I've ever received.

In *I Chose You*, I talked about my "never" list; never kiss a boy, never get married, never get married again, or again, never live in the Midwest, and never have a dog. I should have included another one last time: Gardening. I am so not a fan of gardening.

Flowers and plants all have meanings and symbolize different things. Take the brilliant yellow goldenrod, for example. Like dogs, goldenrod can thrive in many conditions, and they send a message of positivity and strength, embodying the spirit of moving forward and flourishing despite adversity.

Stories are like seeds we plant in the soil of our lives. When we tell stories, we spark a connection. Pretty much everything I learned about dogs, and about gardening, and even about life in general, came from someone telling me a story.

I am a storyteller, Coconut's mom, and a reluctant gardener. Only one of these three descriptors comes naturally. If you ask anyone in my family, they'll tell you I am also creative, stubborn, and that failure is not an option.

Since my husband and I moved from Hawaii to Wisconsin several years ago, two things have happened: We've created several unique gardens on our property, and I've become a dog mom.

This is not a gardening book, but there are parallels in dogs and gardening. I've learned that they both help to create order from chaos and beauty from pain. Dogs and gardening teach us that if we work at it, life can be better than just okay.

I hope you enjoy the wide variety of dogs and the people whose lives have been changed because they rescued a four-legged companion.

CHAPTER ONE

DAFFODIL
NEW BEGINNINGS

POSITIVE CHANGES

"Well I do find the beauty in animals. I find beauty everywhere.
I find beauty in my garden."
— Doris Day

I was sixty-two when we moved to Wisconsin from Hawaii after I experienced a traumatic brain injury. My son and his family lived here, and that is why we chose Oshkosh. We bought an 1875 two-story home after a quick tour in September. We closed in January, moved in March, and had no idea of how much work this old house needed. Or the yard.

When I was growing up in a family with eight kids, we all had specific jobs. My oldest brother was tasked with mowing the yard and keeping the weeds at bay. Kevin, the one with a million ideas, decided to get something to take care of a chore he obviously did not enjoy.

I don't know exactly where he got the weed killer, but, knowing Kevin, it could easily have "fallen off a truck" or it could have been from his fast-talking ways. He always was a bit of a con artist, that brother of mine.

I guess Kevin figured that if it called for a little bit, then a lot would work better. He was liberal with the stuff and it killed every bit of grass. Only dirt was left. In the spring we had mud, in the summer we had dust, and when the snow melted, we had another round of mud. Anyone who tried to grow flowers quickly learned that it was an inhospitable environment for all but the heartiest of weeds.

Our new yard in Wisconsin wasn't nearly as inhospitable as the one at my childhood home, but at times it sure felt like it was. Despite knowing nothing about gardening, and not having the funds to hire someone, we've managed to tame our savage yard.

It's been seven years since the first spring and summer we moved to Wisconsin and tried to figure the easiest and cheapest way to create beauty in our new environment. We've completed countless home improvement projects and somehow found the money to pay for them.

I know I could never have accomplished what I have if it had not been for adopting Coconut. He gave me a purpose and taught me that while change can be harder as we age, it's not impossible.

Our second gardening year, I decided we needed to design a space for the early spring flowers. Gary about killed himself unearthing massive boulders and amending the soil for the daffodil and tulip bulbs. He'll be the first to admit he was not happy about the project. Now, of course, he loves seeing the new growth each spring, signaling a new beginning after a long and gloomy winter.

The daffodils' cheerful and optimistic appearance remind me of new beginnings and that I need to embrace the opportunities and possibilities that come with each new day. My dog was rescued from a high-kill shelter in Kentucky and transported here to Wisconsin. We don't know his story. I think he was a runner with no tags or microchip and his family never found him, but there was a lot of change for him as there is for every rescue dog.

I can imagine how scared Coconut must have been to be away from his person in a strange place with a cacophony of deafening barks and howls. Thanks to the many people involved the rescue and adoption, thousands of dogs each year experience new beginnings filled with hope and optimism.

When we moved here, I kind of felt like Coconut must have felt. I didn't know anyone, I had done practically no research about the area, and I truly did not want to be alive. Coconut and gardening, to a lesser extent, made my new life better every day.

When I did marketing and related tasks for NEW PAWSibilities we had a large number of adopters who were old enough to get AARP notices in the mail. Since I was in that demographic, I enjoyed hearing their stories about why they wanted to adopt. Some were adding a dog while others were, like me, getting their first one. I listened to stories about job loss, health issues, downsizing, and loss of a spouse, just to name a few.

When I decided to write this rescue dog series, I knew one of the books would include stories from people like me who were moving into a new stage of life. The cool thing about dogs is that they don't care about your age; every word in this book could have been written by someone in any decade of life.

Being a dog mom and helping an independent shelter rescue find homes for over 6,500 dogs was not a life goal. I didn't even want to own a dog, and I sure didn't want to garden. But life happens. I can honestly say that my pooch and the spaces we have created have been equally healing in ways I could never have imagined.

A SURPRISING SOUVENIR
Andrea Hunter

"A dog is like a person – he needs a job and a family
to be what he's meant to be."
— Andrew Vachss

I told everyone, including myself, that the last thing I wanted was another dog, after going through the pain of losing our beloved Weimaraner, Sukie. She was as mischievous and high-strung as they come. I'm not going to lie; we'd had quite a rocky start. Once we figured things out, Sukie became my shadow. The winter she passed away left me devastated. I couldn't allow myself or my family to endure that kind of grief again, so I established a new rule: no more dogs.

But as the saying goes, some rules are made to be broken.

It was the summer before our son's senior year of high school—the perfect time to visit the college he planned to attend out west. Our oldest daughter had already left the nest, so perhaps this trip was an effort for us to create new memories as a family. Before anyone could protest too loudly, the truck was loaded and we were enroute for a good old-fashioned family road trip.

Thirteen hundred miles of highway stretched between our sleepy little village in Illinois and our ultimate destination in Montana. We decided to make the most of every mile. From a family photo-op under the legendary fifty-five-foot-tall Jolly Green Giant in Blue Earth, Minnesota, to the obligatory "free" ice water at Wall Drug in South Dakota, we hit every well-known landmark as well as a few of the lesser knowns. The trip out was epic in every possible way. After a promising college visit, we began what I assumed would be a slow-paced, uneventful journey home.

We were about seven hours from Deadwood, South Dakota, where we had arranged to meet with a family friend. Spending a few days with him in the old town would be an excellent way to break up the miles and have a little fun. After watching a parade and the rodeo one evening, our friend asked if we'd like to visit a local resort with him the next day. Nestled in the Black Hills, it boasts incredible views that he thought we would enjoy.

South Dakota is a beautiful place; how could we resist? So, the following day, we piled into the truck and made our way out of town, twisting through heavily wooded ridges and daring bends in the road until we arrived at the resort. He was right; the views were truly breathtaking.

The kids and I were content to explore the grounds while my husband and our friend went inside to chat with his former business associate who had recently left his life of agriculture and farming to run the resort. Nothing could have prepared me for what came next.

I had just settled into my seat to wait for their return when my husband, looking more animated than I had seen him look the whole trip, urgently tapped his knuckle on the truck's passenger window.

"Hey, honey, you've got to get out here and see this dog."

My brain tried to wrap itself around his sudden appearance, holding a leash with a wildly furry, rather rambunctious animal at the other end. Our friend stood back a few paces in the parking lot with his former business partner, both wearing hopeful grins. Not the least bit suspicious.

I rolled down the window and yelled, maybe a bit louder than necessary, "Is that an Irish wolfhound?"

"It is if you want her to be," said the former-farmer-turned-resort-owner. I head a smugness that let me know something was planned that I was not going to like.

"I don't understand. What exactly is going on here?"

"Well, I can't take care of her anymore," answered Mr. Resort Guy. "She's a good dog. Just ask your husband. But she's a runner and needs space, which I no longer have since we moved to town. Although I hate to give her up, she's got a real gift for hunting pheasant."

He looked at my husband. "You've seen her at work a few times; isn't she the best bird dog? If you guys don't take her, well, I just don't know what else to do."

Skepticism gave way to crystal clear understanding. I had been set up.

"The best, really?" I looked at my husband, who had a sheepish grin spreading across his reddened face.

"She's really good, that's for sure. And for the record, she's not a wolfhound; she's a wirehaired pointing griffon." Now he was the hopeful one. He quickly added, "Her name is Penny. Isn't she adorable?"

I had to admit that she was adorable.

The kids had already jumped out to greet her, instantly on board with bringing her home. "Pleeeease, Mom," they chimed in unison. If I didn't know better, I might've assumed they were part of the scheme from the start.

I still felt quite dubious about being duped. But when I stepped down from my perch to meet her, Penny greeted me with the kindest eyes and a sweetness that melted my dog-hardened heart.

"What do you say? Can you take her?" Fully supported by my husband, the kids, and our friend, the city slicker with not enough room for a hunting dog to roam looked at me. He was the perfect picture of innocence. Even Penny seemed to be anticipating my answer. How could I say no?

Today, the kids are all grown, and while Penny might be slowing down just a bit, she still loves to run. And I couldn't be happier to have been tricked into such a surprising souvenir.

A NEW LIFE WITH BABY
Tricia Stertz as told by Herb Doemel

"Puppies are nature's remedy for feeling unloved,
plus numerous other ailments of life."
— Richard Allen Palm

As I was walking down the church aisle, I looked with concern at one of our widowed senior citizens. Even though it was a bright, sunny, Sunday morning, Herb was slightly slumped in his aisle seat, walker and oxygen tank at his side, struggling to keep his eyes open.

I crouched at his side to make eye contact and gently touch his arm.

"Are you feeling okay, Herb? You look really tired."

Herb roused himself and gave a short laugh. "Oh, I'm fine. It's that new puppy I have—she's been keeping me awake!"

"You have a new puppy?" I asked with a burst of astonishment. "This I have to hear."

He was only too happy to share his story with me. Herb's earlier years were idyllic at his family's lakeside home surrounded by friends, cousins, and carefree play. Then, the unexpected happened; His father bought a large farm, moved them to the country, and his perfect life was suddenly gone.

He was the youngest and, without any friends to play with, Herb felt like an only child. He was sad and discouraged. But as a part of the farm purchase, they inherited two goats, a turkey hen, and a collie/shepherd mix named Shep who became his friend and companion.

Farming is hard work and not something Herb aspired to do. Instead, he secured a job at Rockwell Standard, married, and had two children. He enjoyed his life, but as happens to all, sorrows and tragedy struck.

Not long after he achieved his long-anticipated retirement, his beloved wife, June, was diagnosed with ovarian cancer. Herb wanted to make her final years as rewarding as possible and asked her what she really would like. June said, "I've always thought it would be nice to raise puppies."

Over the years Herb and June had a consistent parade of small dogs with Herb taking on the bulk or their care. Even though it was more work for him, he fell in love with them all. When June decided she wanted to raise puppies, Herb said yes.

After the diagnosis, Herb and June got a male and two female shih tzus and had eight litters. June kept meticulous records over the eight years they raised and sold puppies to those who wanted to buy from a responsible breeder.

Sadly, June was getting weaker as her disease robbed her energy. The last of the puppies were sold, and she spent much more time sleeping. Herb told June that he was lonely during those long hours, and she said that what he really needed was to get a dog for himself.

June started searching and found one she thought would be perfect for him. Despite being sick and weak, she insisted on driving with him to pick up a dog to be his companion. They drove to a remote farm and that's where Suzy, the shih tzu puppy, became part of their family.

Herb says Suzy was a perfect dog and a good companion. When June died in 2000, Suzy was constantly with him. Herb bought a three-wheeler with a basket on the front, and Suzy would trot with him for miles while he pedaled. She would politely ask for a ride in the basket when she got tired.

But that day when I stopped by Herb's side at church, he told me Suzy was already sixteen years old, her joints were old and stiff, and she was slowing down. She had always jumped on his bed and slept with him, but lately, he had to help her up. He knew she would not be with him much longer, and he couldn't imagine his life without a dog.

He started thinking about getting another pup, and then he noticed an ad in the newspaper for a miniature Pomeranian puppy. The same advertisement was in the paper for several weeks, and Herb couldn't get it off his mind. His daughter agreed to drive him to see the puppy, even though it was hours away on the far west side of the state.

Trying to follow the directions, they were almost convinced they were completely on the wrong track as they wandered down miles of poorly marked, gravel roads. When they finally drove into the yard, there she was: a petite, pure-white Pomeranian, with just a little brownish ring around her eyes and ears.

Herb knew immediately that this was the pup for him. He was convinced that God had led him to this particular dog. When the paperwork was done, Herb's new two-pound puppy, whom he named Baby, was on her way home.

Suzy was always calm and sweet, content, and never barked. But this new little upstart was the opposite. She would jump on Suzy's back, ruffle her fur, and chew on her ears. From the start, Baby barked like a guard dog and held her long tail in a curlicue, tight around her back, and loved chasing it. Herb says she still chases in vain, but has never been successful.

This was the little dynamo that was keeping Herb awake, causing me to pause and check on him in church. When I talked to Herb on the phone this afternoon, he told me that Suzy passed on last week. In his voice I heard his sadness at her passing. I was about to mention how sorry I was for his loss when, in the background, I heard the boisterous sound of the little Pomeranian.

"Yup, that's Baby." There was an enthusiastic lilt to his voice. "Can you hear her? I love that little dog!"

THE COOL MOM

"Life begins the day you start a garden."
— Chinese Proverb

I would be lying if I said our yard looks like it does today because we had a passion for native plants. When the snow finally melted after we moved to this house in March of 2017, we learned we had a flooding problem. And then it snowed again, and for three more weeks, our trash and recycle bins were frozen solid onto the apron. This led to more flooding when the thaw started.

At that point we didn't know that very little in the back yard was salvageable. We did find out that the massive cracks in our garage floor were because of years of flooding each spring. And then something wonderful happened.

Through our neighborhood association I learned about rain garden grants available through the Oshkosh Southwest Rotary. A rain garden is, at its core, an area that collects rainwater, holds it for a limited amount of time, and filters it before slowly releasing the water into the ground. I could tell you a bunch more about rain gardens, but the important part is that ours is planted with native grasses and flowering perennials, which has reduced runoff from our yard and eliminated the flooding.

Our back yard was perfectly suited for this project, provided we figured out a way to get more sun. We had these messy, and not particularly attractive, pine trees blocking the sun and breeze from our yard. We also had a cherry tree that had been struck by lighting and would never do much except take up space. Down came the trees one noisy day, and we started the process of preparing for the coming garden.

They say a weed is just a plant growing in a place where it's not meant to be. I call them invaders. We discovered that our yard was at least ninety-five percent invaders. Gary and I were total gardening rookies, but we did connect with a nursery that helped us choose the right mix of native grasses and flowers.

After preparing the space, had I known how much work it was going to be, I'm not sure we would have gone this route. We received live plants via two-day delivery. I learned they are called plugs, and they came with a spread sheet and a sort of diagram of where to put them. And then we prayed. I had never spent so much money in my life on living things that could die. Not even my kids.

We had a health maintenance organization (HMO) insurance plan when my son was born. Thanks to that, he cost a whopping five dollars. You read that right. From the day I learned I was pregnant until the day I brought him home, that was the total cost. The first phase of the garden was $1,000.

The grant was for $500, so I figured we'd only be down $500 if everything died. Every plant bloomed, and it went so well that we added phase two the next season. Now we have bees, butterflies, birds, and insects—and nature is in healing right in our back yard. And miracle of all miracles, the flooding issue was solved.

We've gone on to remove lots of grass and add more pollinator gardens in both the front and back yard. In the beginning of the summer my son and his family came over to see the garden for the first time this year.

"Mom, you really do have a pollinator garden," exclaimed my son when he saw the rain garden. "This is great. I never knew anyone who did this in their yard."

At that moment I was once again the cool mom. The mom who baked the best cookies, the one who bought a basketball hoop because that meant all the kids came to my house to hang out. I was the mom who devised the ideas for school projects, who let my boys ride their bikes wherever they chose in our little town as long as they didn't go to the beach. Then they became teenagers, and I wasn't the cool mom any more.

But all of the sudden I was not only the cool mom, but the cool grandma. The look on my five-year-old grandson's face when he saw the size of this garden was worth every penny we paid, every weed we pulled, and every moment of doubt. Our flooding is gone, we have drought-resistant gardens, I can't even begin to count the number of bees in our yard each day—and, once again, I am the cool mom.

I also have a dog named Coconut. My son and his wife have busy schedules and a small house with an unfenced yard. They have decreed that the boys cannot have a dog or a cat. I'm thinking this is another way I can be the cool grandma.

I read somewhere that the worst mistake a gardener can make is to think that he or she is in charge. My relative success as a gardener is because I realized that there are things I can't control. Like the amount of rain or snow we have, whether our neighbors keep their weeds in check (they don't), or if we have enough sunny days. However, I *can* control many things. I can prepare the ground correctly, weed, fertilize and prune as suggested, and then weed some more. So much weeding.

I think the same can be said about having a dog. We rescued my dog when he was fourteen months old. I didn't know his past, if he had any genetic health issues, or even his true breed mix. I enrolled him in a six-week training class—which is really for the humans, if the truth be told—I fed him the right kind of food, I gave him exercise and a ton of love. Pretty much the same things I did with my two-legged sons.

Many of the plants are rescue plants. You'll read about some of them and how they came to live in our yard. Rescue plants and dogs have a lot of similarities. In some ways I think dogs are easier.

If anyone needs hope, here it is. I was a Wisconsin transplant, had never gardened, was brain damaged, and had a really stinky attitude. I had also never owned my own dog.

American horticulturist Liberty Hyde Bailey said, "A garden requires patient labor and attention. Plants do not grow merely to satisfy ambitions or to fulfill good intentions. They thrive because someone expended effort on them."

The same can be said about dogs. Six years into being a reluctant gardener and an even more unwilling dog mom have taught me that each day is a new adventure.

A TORNADO ON FOUR PAWS
Kristine Lowder

"A dog's heart is bigger than any 'thing' you can ever own."
— Elizabeth Parker

We live in a small rural town in Washington state where the local economy is sluggish at best. Because of the lack of career opportunities here, two of my sons moved out last summer to pursue their dreams. One followed a job offer to South Carolina, which was the end of the world in "mom speak." The other joined the navy; the other end of the world in the previously noted language.

"We knew you'd be sad, Mom," said Nathan and Sam, explaining why they chose to keep their plans an eleventh-hour surprise. "We didn't want to upset you more with long goodbyes."

I guess sons have a different definition of the word "long," because by the time Sam shared about his plans, I had a mere ten days to process the news and do all the things a mom does when her son is leaving. It was even worse with Nathan. In less than forty-eight hours, he'd be starting his new life.

A number of my friends were counting the sands in the hourglass until they could call themselves empty nesters. They insisted that the joys were many—including freedom, solitude, and the ability to pack up and go any time they felt footloose and fancy free.

After my sons packed their belongings and set off for their new lives, all I heard was the eerie curtain of quiet that suddenly settled over the house. The empty rooms etched with decades of memories. Echoes of laughter and love. The sudden quiet wrapped around my heart like a funeral shroud.

The dual departure was unexpectedly abrupt. If I'd had more time to adjust to the whole empty nest thing, it may not have hit me so hard. But the suddenness left me feeling bereft, as if I had been tossed into the spin cycle of an emotional washing machine.

Thinking of life without my boys brought back the memory of the best dog I'd ever owned, even though it had been ten years since she had left me. Eve, a gentle yellow Lab with a coat the color of toasted marshmallows and the personality of Pooh Bear, changed my world when she bounded into my life as a young adult dog.

Eve thought everyone was her best friend. She wasn't wrong. She brought out the best in and thought the best of everyone. She was loyal, loving, and generous. Even when every other family member scattered to the four winds with work, school, sports, or other pursuits, I was never alone. There was always Eve, a palomino sirocco on four feet.

The day she died was one of the worst days of my life, one I thought I'd never survive. But I did. And I would survive my empty nest. But this time, my survival would include the love of a different dog

Three years after Eve's death, my friend Deb sent me a photo of an adoptable puppy from a local dog rescue organization. She was awfully cute. I hesitated. After all, there could never be another Eve. Besides, she was a puppy.

"How old is she?" I messaged Deb.

"She's ten weeks old. Up to date on all her vaccinations. House and leash-trained."

For the previous three years whenever I'd flirted with the idea of getting a dog, my constant refrain had been that I did not want a puppy. I'd never had a puppy before—only adult dogs. I was wary about getting such a young pooch, mostly because I didn't know a thing about training and all that entailed. It seemed so daunting.

I looked at the photo of the adorable border collie/mix and my heart melted a bit. Where Eve was the color of honey and sunshine, this pup was black and white. Maybe, just maybe, a puppy wouldn't be nearly the work others had described. I'd raised my sons to be functioning adults; how much harder could a puppy be?

"Would you like to meet at the park?" Deb asked. "I'll bring her, and you can get acquainted. We'll go from there."

"Would you like to hold her?" asked Deb as soon as we connected.

I took her into my arms and turned to mush in about a nanosecond. That's how the smartest member of the family joined us after all the requisite adoption paperwork was completed. And I got a crash course in raising and training a puppy.

Kimber hasn't left my side since, joyously greeting each new day with her Kimber-patented "I love everyone; ain't life grand?' effervescence. When my sons moved out to begin new careers, Kimber seemed to sense my distress. Her bubbly personality rescued me from my despondency and buoyed my sagging spirits. She lifted me up with her unconditional love and eternal optimism.

Just as Eve never left me alone, neither did Kimber. On days when I didn't want to get up, Kimber gently nudged me awake, prodded me out of bed, and got me out of the house. She'd wait patiently next to her leash for our walk. Once we ventured outside, Kimber persuaded me to play ball or toss the frisbee, to work in the garden, and to take long walks on the beach.

On days when I didn't feel like going out because I was thinking about my sons and missing them mightily, Kimber insisted otherwise. Together, we re-connected with friends and neighbors.

If Eve was the scirocco on four feet, then Kimber outdoes her energy and enthusiasm and is a tornado on four paws. I doubt I would've had the motivation to do any of the above if it hadn't been for Kimber. I soon started listening for the welcoming bark of my best girl, the jangle of her dog tags. I delighted in watching her ears perk up at the sound of my voice. Knowing that Kimber's warm, amber eyes follow my every move gives me hope and joy.

DAWDLE AND SNIFF

*"I'll believe it if I see it" for dogs translates to
"I'll believe it if I smell it."*
— Cesar Millan with Melissa Jo Peltier

For many years, I lived in a state where the local news had no weather person. Most of the time we lived in the land of the '70s, with plenty of sun and gorgeous trade winds. At the end of each broadcast the anchor recapped the day, telling us it was a low of 72 and a high of 77, 20 miles per hour trade winds, and more like that tomorrow. If something hovered like a hurricane or a tropical storm, it wasn't weather because it was news. And mainland snow storms or forest fires? Those were news and only mattered if we had family in those areas or if they caused travel delays to and from the islands.

I moved away for nine years, and when I came back, all the stations had hired weather people. Nothing had changed—Hawaii was still the land of the '70s—but the powers that be decided that the news had to include full weather reports and green screen maps.

Then we moved to Wisconsin where weather is the main event unless the Packers are playing. There are four distinct dog-walking seasons; snow and too cold, rain and mud, enjoyable (this season is way too short), and then there's a period of time when it's all mixed into one day. Just when you are starting to lose hope that you and your dog will ever be able to enjoy walking together, the skies clear and the temperatures become unseasonably warm.

A week before Thanksgiving was one of those sunny, dry, and almost 60-degree days. Coconut and I walked for well over an hour. We walked with a friend and laughed and talked, saw more dogs and their owners, and felt like maybe, maybe, it would not be a brutal winter. As we were solving all the world's problems—'cause that's what seniors do as we walk and talk—my friend made an observation.

"You sure don't get your heart racing when you're walking that dog," he noted.

I explained that when I decided to get a dog, I had visions of a well-trained pooch who was a champion leash walker. I figured by walking at least five or more fast-paced miles a day, my pounds would melt off. That didn't happen.

Our fast-paced walks are more like dawdling while this mutt of mine goes from side to side, sniffing, marking, and, ever so often, pooping. Then he finds new territory and runs over to sniff as if he has found buried treasure or a decomposing body. Nope. Just smelling for something we humans will never understand.

One thing I learned early during life with Coconut is that most people are usually all about the destination, while dogs care more about the journey. There's a lesson in there. When my life becomes frantic then I need to be more like Coconut.

According to the American Kennel Club, it's no wonder that dogs are all about sniffing, since they have over roughly forty times more smell-sensitive receptors than humans, ranging from about 125 million to nearly 300 million in some breeds, such as bloodhounds.

By taking my pooch on a sniff-centric walk, I let him decide which direction, how long he wants to linger, and where he wants to go next. I have to keep my eyes peeled to the ground so that I can redirect him if he finds a pizza crust or even a chicken bone. Today was chicken bone day but he's good about the drop it command.

Except when the weather is extreme, we walk. I let him greet the neighborhood dogs, I chat with random people who are also enjoying or braving the weather, and he'll dawdle and sniff and mark because he takes his job of being a dog very seriously.

When the snow melts for a time, or the rain washes the old smells away, Coconut is oblivious of my discomfort as he takes his time sniffing and enjoying life as only a dog can. My job is to remember how much I love him and to wear layers and good gloves.

CHARLIE'S SONG
Michele Miles Gardiner

"Dogs teach us a very important lesson in life:
The mailman is not to be trusted"
— Sian Ford

"We wonder where Charlie came from," I told the pet psychic over the phone. Our little white Maltese/mix tilted his head as he heard his name. My husband, Ian, and I wanted to learn about our dog. Hey, don't judge.

Had it been my money, maybe I would not have made the call. But if you had a parent who suggested, "A pet psychic would be fun! I'll pay," that would likely change things, as it did for us.

We met Charlie on a rainy November day in 2014. Ian was on our driveway when a car pulled up to our house. A woman got out of the car and approached him. She held a small dog with wet, matted fur.

"This dog yours?" The woman asked him.

"No."

"Are you sure?

"Uh, yeah!

"Well, if you don't want it, I'm taking it to the animal shelter."

Ian, usually the person in our family who admonished our daughter Lauren and me with the words, "No more animals," took the soaking dog into our house.

We spent the next month trying to find the dog's home. Nobody claimed him. We fell in love with the little guy and named him Charlie.

Ian said the woman who left Charlie seemed off-kilter. He suspected Charlie was her dog, and she wanted to dump him.

Back to the pet psychic part of the story. She told us Charlie thinks his previous human companion was "a kooky lady," and not in a good way. Also, Charlie believes he has a good sense of humor. Good thing, considering all that he's been through with us.

Soon after he became part of our family, Charlie accompanied Lauren as she left our Los Angeles-area home to attend San Francisco State University. She stayed with my parents, living in a cottage behind their house in the Bay Area. They welcomed Charlie, too. As Lauren's college roommate, Charlie calmed her during stressful studying, kept her company, and, when allowed, sat with her in classes.

After his college days, Charlie returned to live with Ian and me as Lauren found an apartment and began working.

Over the years, we've gotten to know a lot about our dog with an enormous spirit in his tiny body.

The second he sees me put on shoes, he becomes a dancer—wiggling his bottom and tapping his feet, practically shouting, "It's happening. We're going for a walk!" As if leading a conga line—one, two, cha-cha-cha—he heads for the front door.

He's also a Zen master—sitting in the sun, worry-free; sniffing flowers—not fretting about the past or the future. If Charlie could speak, he'd say, "It's all about now, man."

However, that's not the case if it's almost his dinner time and Charlie sees me doing something other than preparing his food. Then he'd say, "Hey, Ms. Easily Distracted! It's my food time."

As for bedtime, if it's after 11 p.m., he'll corral Ian and me toward the bedroom—doesn't matter if I'm reading or if Ian's on his computer. Charlie walks to the bedroom, pauses to look back, and gives us the stink eye for not following. He'll blow out a frustrated "Hmpff," before jumping on the bed.

While he may look like a walking coconut cupcake with big black raisin eyes, he imagines himself a tough guy—protecting our house as if he's a security guard for the mafia. Charlie growls and froths in a mad frenzy when the mailman dares to invade our doorway. One day, after his vicious warnings to the postal worker, I heard an explosion of shattering glass. Charlie had burst through our front window and chased the mailman down the street. Thankfully, the only thing harmed was the glass.

We love coming home to see Charlie waiting at our front window (now repaired with thicker glass). He jumps up and down, head back, howling with happiness. Charlie loves it when Ian walks through the door and bends down to give him scratches. That's their thing—guy bonding.

But Charlie said, "Things are different now," the pet psychic told us during that call in 2022.

After a stunned pause, I said, "Wow. Well . . . Ian had a stroke in 2020. So our lives changed. When we became busy with Ian's physical therapy, Charlie didn't get as many walks. Ian was in a wheelchair for a while, so Charlie didn't get his chin scratched at the door."

Our little guy became our emotional support dog.

Charlie would jump up and sit on Ian's stroke-affected left side. He'd lick Ian's face and arm, giving him love and comfort.

Before that, when Ian was in the hospital and physical therapy rehab for a month, Charlie licked away my tears and snuggled with me as I slept alone. Charlie no longer did his happy dance to walk when I put on shoes. He knew. Things were different.

Ian's health has improved, so Charlie's getting his chin scratched at the door again.

Because Ian's a musician, our home is filled with musical instruments—basses, guitars, and a piano—great physical therapy for his brain and finger muscle connections. Recently, he composed a song on the piano for Charlie. Ian and I have been married for thirty-four years, but he has never written a song for me. Maybe I need to do a happy dance at the window when he comes home.

Anyway, it's a beautiful melody. At night, Ian sits at the piano and begins playing Charlie's song. Our dog prances over to the piano to watch and hear Ian play. He wags his tail. I sit on the floor and pet Charlie, singing the lyrics we have so far.

"Charlie, the Wonder Dog. We wonder where you came from. We wonder if you know how much we love you. Charlie, you're wonderful. We wonder how we got so lucky. Charlie, the Wonder Dog. . . . "

The lyrics need work. But so do we. I'm sure Charlie thinks we're kooky. Thankfully, he has a sense of humor. Well, that's what he told the psychic.

TEARS FOR NATALIE
Janice Thompson

"Fall in love with a dog, and in many ways, you enter a new orbit, a universe that features not just new colors but new rituals, new rules, a new way of experiencing attachment."
— Caroline Knapp

In December of 2002, my life changed forever. It started with an email from a dear friend, letting me know of a seven-week-old beagle mix pup that needed a good home. I didn't respond to her email . . . simply wasn't interested.

I went to visit my friend the next weekend. It was completely innocent, really. We were simply meeting for dinner and quiet conversation. Nothing about dogs in the mix. Until I laid eyes on Natalie.

An amazing thing happens when you find the perfect puppy, something undeniable. A bonding takes place. It's unexplainable, really, but I now speak from first-hand experience. On December 7, 2002, I fell in love with a beagle pup named Natalie and my world would never be the same. As I drove home with this tiny bundle curled up in my fleece jacket, I whispered a little prayer: "Why? Why did you give me this little dog instead of the one I wanted?"

In my heart I heard the following response: "Sometimes we don't get what we want. Sometimes we get what we need." I didn't understand those words then, but I do now.

My family fell in love with Natalie immediately, just as I had. This tiny beagle babe was everything a family could want—good natured, quiet, and loving. We had made the perfect choice. However, our definition of "perfect" was about to be challenged.

Within a matter of days, we knew Natalie had a problem. She struggled to walk and kept toppling over into her food bowl. She would tilt her head and tremor on occasion. I prayed this was normal puppy behavior, but knew in my heart it was not. The next three weeks were riddled with visits to the vet. The diagnosis was grim, to say the least.

Neurological problems.

Frankly, I'd never heard of such a thing in puppies, but Natalie was suffering from a neurological condition called Cerebellar Hypoplasia. Pups with this problem have under-developed cerebellums. Since this area of the brain controls motor skills, Natalie's ability to walk normally and consistently would never improve. Interestingly enough, it would probably never get any worse, either.

I'm not a "crier." However, I wept like a baby all the way home from the Animal Clinic. Natalie never knew the difference. She slept soundly, curled up on my chest. But my heart would not stop breaking. This just seemed too unfair, for her and for us.

At first, we really struggled to know what to do. Friends and loved ones encouraged us to euthanize the puppy quickly, but we couldn't let go that easily. "Don't get too attached," they said.

Too late. We were head over heels in love. Of course, we didn't want to see her suffer, but we didn't want to give up hope, either. The questions to be answered were, "How much can Natalie live with?" and "How much can we live with?" At the vet's suggestion, we decided to wait until she reached sixteen weeks of age before making any decisions one way or the other. At that point, we knew we should keep going.

Natalie didn't appear to be in any pain and the episodes of falling, along with some tremors, were mirrored with hours of typical puppy behavior. Other than the obvious struggles, she could lead a relatively normal life, depending on your definition of normal.

Natalie lived to be eighteen months old before crossing the rainbow bridge, but those eighteen months changed my life forever and gave me a passion to focus my attention on dogs in need. From that day until now, I've fostered over fifty dogs and adopted enough to fill a pet shop.

My tears have dried up now. Hope has resurrected and the future looks bright—for all of us. Natalie was the catalyst, the pet God used to teach me how to love passionately, to think creatively, and to intervene as often as possible.

Puppy love is more than just a silly crush. It's a dedicated, life-long commitment to care for an animal, regardless of its flaws. Through the tears. Through the unknown. It's an acknowledgement that perfection is found in the eye of the beholder.

And we beheld perfection every time we looked into Natalie's sweet face.

CHAPTER TWO

BLACK-EYED SUSANS
RESILIENCE

MATT'S MEMORY GARDEN

"You have to get up and plant the seed and see if it grows, but you can't just wait around, you have to water it and take care of it."
— Bootsy Collins

I first met Matt when he was around twenty-years-old. I'd seen pictures, but nothing prepared me for that smile and those incredibly kind eyes of his.

I had to look down on him, not because I was so much taller, but because he was in a wheelchair. While my two healthy and active sons played basketball and soccer and rode bikes throughout their mom-approved boundaries, Matt struggled to walk pain-free. Psoriatic arthritis was something I had only heard about from the commercials featuring professional golfer Phil Mickelson. Yet that was what Matt dealt with each day.

His life up until that point included a rod in his back and many, many trips to the specialists at Boston's Children Hospital. Arthritis and the cold, wet, Massachusetts weather are not the best of friends. His father decided moving with him to Florida made sense, and they hoped the weather would help.

I was caring for my late husband, David, who had Huntington's disease when Gary and Matt entered our lives. Since I was already in caregiver mode, I began helping Matt with diet, exercise, and finding a good doctor. We all cheered as Matt went from a wheelchair to a walker and then to a cane. Matt's improvement dovetailed with my husband's decline. We knew David's situation was terminal, but we looked forward to Matt's continued improvement.

It's a long saga, but despite reaching some wonderful milestones, Matt decided to move back to New England. Family was everything to him, and he felt that the extra special times with his nieces and nephews made the move worth every ounce of pain.

I eventually married Gary, and he and I and others tried unsuccessfully to sway Matt from his decision because the weather and not having doctors or a good routine would be hard on his body. He was determined to leave the sun for the cold and went from that cane to the walker and, in a shorter time than imaginable, to being bedridden.

Matt was living in a nursing home in 2020 during that crazy time when family members weren't allowed to visit after the pandemic began. However, one sneaky and incredibly unwanted visitor snuck in: COVID-19. Despite the heroic efforts of his medical team, a little over a week after he tested positive, Matt passed away—a few days shy of his forty-fourth birthday.

Like with too many others during that time, there was no funeral, no memorial, no family gathering from around the country to celebrate his life. No meals prepared and eaten as stories were told, laughter mingled with tears, and hugs to comfort everyone who loved this sweet, gentle young man with the happy smile and sparkly eyes.

Gary and I decided to create Matt's hope and healing garden as a lasting memorial to him. We prepared the soil—no easy feat—and planted a native grass and four different varieties of black-eyed Susans, one of the first flowers to come back after times of flood, fire, and other times of calamity.

Coconut loves to be with us when we are all together out in the sun. Maybe it was his way of encouraging us to make it through all of the pea gravel and weeds, but he was content to play and sleep and be on the lookout for squirrels and bunnies instead of pestering us for a walk.

Last year we took out more grass and weeds, always a good thing, and planted native grasses and added a walkway fashioned from flagstone and bricks painted by grandkids and friends. We added a bench to sit and rest amongst those happy flowers that never fail to make me smile. They are like dogs in that way.

Black-Eyed Susans have long been associated with resilience, motivation, and positive change which are all perfect for a book about rescue dogs. Before we adopted Coconut and I started volunteering, I never thought about what a tough life too many of them have. Thanks to all of the rescuers and families who open their homes and their hearts our pooches are as happy as the flowers in our memory garden.

On a sunny yellow entryway wall in our home are two professionally framed canvas prints. The one we purchased in Matt's memory is a field of wildflowers below a pink-hued sky, shot with golden shafts of light. I believe that Matt is in heaven, and he's running in a field of flowers on two legs—pain-free as he never was in life. His wheelchair is gone.

Running alongside of Matt is his childhood dog, Tippy. She's young and carefree and the two of them are happy and healthy. Matt never got to meet my dog. But I bet if all dogs really do go to heaven, then Coconut and Tippy will be great friends when Coconut gets there. And they'll both lick Matt's face as they roll around in the wildflowers.

On cold winter nights, I curl up on the sofa with a heavy throw to ward off the cold. My little dog sits by my feet, and across from me I see the wildflower print and, next to it, a stunning photo of black-eyed Susans in honor of our neighbor who passed away just a few years after we moved here. They remind me that the cold of winter isn't year-round, that the sun always comes up, and that I'm a better person because of my dog.

POLLY THE GRUNTING PIG DOG

*"Sometimes the smallest things take up
the most room in your heart."*
— A.A.Milne

Pat is a cat person, always has been. She didn't dislike dogs, but she'd only owned cats and always thought that would be the case. The "best laid plans" and all that is how this story begins.

An acquaintance of Pat's told her that he had found a free dog in need of a home. Tom wanted a lapdog and, from the sound of it, the one he wanted to meet would be the perfect companion. Without doing any other research, off he went to pick up the pup.

She was a cinnamon-colored, short-haired Chihuahua named Polly. Pat and her daughter Jenny went over to meet her, and Jenny fell head over heels in love. Pat explained that dogs are fine, but that they were a cat family, and that's the way it was going to stay.

Tom said that Polly had been kept in deplorable conditions. There had been too many unwashed animals and the home reeked of urine and other smells. Polly never got a chance to be play because she was carried everywhere by the little boy in the family.

One day Tom needed someone to watch Polly. After Pat agreed to dog sit, he brought over fuzzy blankets, a few toys, and some food and treats all meant for a much larger dog. Tom said it would be fine since Polly probably wouldn't eat much. He also suggested that if they had to leave the house, it would be best to shut her in the bathroom in case she had an accident.

They watched in horror as Polly struggled to chew the too-large food. The poor girl could not even get the treat in her little mouth. Pat and Jenny went to the store and got the right-sized food and treats for her.

When they got back home from their trip, they went in to check on how Polly was doing in the bathroom. She'd had an accident which was to be expected. What wasn't expected or appreciated was that she had torn up the vinyl tile floor. Pat decided she would use a cat kennel going forward to put her in when they left the house.

A few days later, Pat called Tom about when she should have Polly ready for pick up. After a brief silence, Tom said that they had decided that Polly wasn't a good fit for them, and they had no intention of coming to get her.

It was quite a surprise, but Pat was not willing to send Polly to the shelter. Pat and Jenny went online to learn how to potty train a dog. They used a cat kennel and got her trained in just a matter of a few days

In her new environment, Polly gobbled down her food and treats and began to add some much-needed pounds to her small frame. Pat called Tom to see if they could get her vet records. Of course she'd never been to a vet, so off they went to for her first shots.

Based on her age, which he estimated to be around seven, the vet told them he thought that she'd probably been a puppy mill breeder until she was of no use to the owners. Her teeth were cavity-ridden and in some cases worn down to the gum line or even missing. She would need to be spayed and have a surgery to fix multiple hernias.

As Polly settled in, she and Tabitha, the eighteen-year-old cat, got along well. Tabitha was the boss, but Polly seemed content with this. One of the funniest quirks of hers was that Polly had a habit of grunting like a pig when she was happy.

Mother and daughter and the pets settled into their lives, and then the unexpected happened. After years of being a single mom, Pat started dating. She told Matt, whom she eventually married, about Polly and how she grunted when she was in her happy space.

Matt refused to believe her because he'd been a dog owner for many years and had never heard of anything so ridiculous. Phone calls and online interactions turned into more time together, and he came over to her house for the first time.

Matt sat on the couch and discovered a fuzzy balled-up blanket next to him. When he patted the lump, he discovered Polly, all rolled up snug as that proverbial bug in the rug. Sure enough, the little Chihuahua, who had survived such a tough life, started grunting like a pig. The shock that filled his face was priceless. Matt could not quit smiling and laughing about Polly, the grunting pig dog.

The couple dated for five years and, eventually, Pat and Jenny and their senior pets moved into Matt's house. Blending families can bring many challenges, but Polly brought unexpected pleasure in another way.

With Polly, Matt's parents have the joy of being grandparents to the sweetest cuddler ever. They had chosen not to have a dog of their own because of the time involved. They adore Polly and they visit often and have started asking Matt and Pat to bring Polly to their house when they come for a visit.

Instead of hiring a dog sitter or paying for boarding when they travel, Polly has sleepovers at Grandma and Grandpa's house. When Pat says they are taking her to stay with her grandparents, Polly gets so excited she tap dances in circles.

Polly is the obvious queen on her visits, and she even sleeps with Grandpa and sits with him on the couch. Of course she rolls up in a fuzzy blanket, because some things never change.

Her snout and teeny little feet are going grey, but her coat is sleek, her appetite is good, and she has made an incredible impact on their blended family.

They say one man's trash is another man's treasure and that is how this story ends. Polly is a treasure and, despite her rough start, she has lived a wonderful life.

GROWING OLD WITH DIOR
Elizabeth Ritzman

"Grow old with me, the best is yet to be!"
— Robert Browning

Once upon a time, I was slaving away as the director of a college health center. I use the word slaving because although I loved my job, there was too much work and not enough time to accomplish it all. The good news is that my team, to a person, all had good sense and good humor and we collaborated well.

We added an instructional component to my managerial role, and I also took on clients as a mental health therapist. You'd think that I would have figured out that it was not smart to continue putting up with the crazy workload. We eventually devised a plan to scale back to a more reasonable spread of duties before we all burned out.

But first came spring break, which meant I was on vacation for more than a couple of days. We'd planned to travel to Virginia to see my son and his family and enjoy a break from the Chicago weather. I couldn't wait.

One of the stress management tools I used when I couldn't sleep at night was to cruise pet search engines where I'd check out all the pups across the country looking for homes. Daisy, our aging coon hound/mix, was totally bonded to my wife, and I wanted my own fur-mate.

Now that a less stressful workload was a real possibility, I became more serious about finding a new pup. Our Daisy had flown over the deck railing after a squirrel and landed six feet below tearing her knee muscle. Poor girl was looking and acting older, and we expected to face the end of her life at some point, especially if she kept being so reckless in the squirrel wars.

As much as I wanted a dog of my own, the odds of that happening were slim. My wife has a very animalistic nature, and she was home most of the time since she'd retired. Animals of every kind gravitate toward her. My scrolling was more a fantasy than a plan.

I had long envied my brother's bond with his Weimaraners, a bird and small prey hunting breed. They are goofy, resilient, and tuned in to their humans, which is what I wanted. While many excellent and caring breeders are out there, I wasn't keen on the potential ethical problems that come with choosing a company or an individual in it for the wrong reasons. And purebred dogs are often prone to medical issues, which I also wanted to avoid.

I kept half an eye out for Weimaraner mixes because while it's possible to find a purebred Weimaraner at a rescue, it's not the norm. One rescue I followed eventually had a few puppies from a full bred Weimaraner who had been a stray in Tennessee. She was rescued in time to have her puppies in a safe, supportive, foster home. I was incredibly tempted and, if I wanted a chance at adopting my dream dog, I had to decide immediately.

I said yes, we would like to meet one of the female puppies. I was on a much-needed vacation when I heard about Lola, who was in foster care with a loving family. We scheduled the date to meet her for when I got back, confident that this might be my girl.

We took off on our trip in March of 2020. Nothing worked out as planned because on the second day of our holiday, Chicago, and pretty much every city in the US, went on lockdown, thanks to COVID–19.

Instead of the relaxing and rejuvenating time we had planned, I was glued to the phone and the computer handling work situations that had no easy solutions. We needed to get home, but we didn't want to risk flying. Dulles was at a standstill, a very crowded one, as we planned to return to Chicago. We wanted to avoid the disaster unfolding in every major airport as travelers struggled to get home or get away, so, after the one-hour trip to pick up a rental car, we headed home.

Never was I more grateful that I had a strong team behind me. The stress of my job multiplied in the most unimagined ways. We didn't have enough staff or a crystal ball to help us plan, but together we made tough decisions while helping some of COVID–19's first victims. I worked all the way from Virginia to Chicago, but as I made lockdown decisions one by one, I instinctively knew I needed to keep my date with Lola.

When we are going through something as monumental as what we all went through those first terrifying weeks of COVID–19, it helps to have something to hope for when things settled down. For me it was my upcoming date to meet a Weimermix puppy.

The pandemic had impacted the rescue world, too. The shelter was locked down when we arrived, and we were instructed to stay in the car until they brought her to us. Pre-COVID–19 meet and greets had taken place inside, with leisurely time to feed the dogs treats, to cuddle, to get to know them a bit. This time around, we had a scared little pup in our truck that was trying to hide from the big coonhound in the back seat.

I begged for ten quiet minutes to see whether this dog had the hoped-for Weimaraner gaze. Most dogs don't hold eye contact for long, if at all, unless you have a treat. This beautiful, long-legged girl gazed unblinkingly into my eyes, and I knew she was my dog.

With her black fur and the white forehead blaze, Lola was the most beautiful dog I'd ever seen and that includes my Great Pyrenees who had passed away. I was already in love with her white paws and tail tip and could not wait to get my girl home.

As hard as lockdown was for all of us, there were a few bright lights and, for me, it was that I had a chance to bond with her and take responsibility for most of her care in those early days. Regardless of the hardships at my work, when I did go to the office, I had a routine of taking her out early, bringing her back in, and dozing in the big chair watching the sun come up. When I came home, I would collapse in that same chair and fall asleep, loving the feel of her nose under my arm. I needed her simple physical warmth and connection badly.

We renamed her Dior, after her elegant Dior-style poise and stature. The connection I hoped would be part of her breed is there; she is my shadow, which never ceases to bring me delight.

I might not have been able to retain my sanity through the that first lockdown and the never-ending pandemic without Dior. Over three years later, I still find myself on edge after the constant emergency during that awful time. At times it's hard to settle down, and I know that Dior has her work cut out for her to keep me settled and improving my relaxation.

Besides finding my dream dog there's more to our happy ending. Retirement is better than I expected. We moved to beautiful Michigan and are enjoying the trails and living life at a much slower pace. I'm getting back into my sewing and other hobbies, and thoughts of the frantic COVID–19 times are fewer and fewer. Some people probably thought adopting a puppy at my age was, let's call it, challenging. To a teeny degree it was. But a puppy means that I will have extra years with Dior and that's worth any of the initial puppy messes and lack of sleep.

I look forward to the two of us growing old together.

OUR FIRST RESCUE PLANTS

"Gardening is an exercise in optimism.
Sometimes, it is a triumph over experience."
— Marina Schinz

The year we started gardening, my neighbor moved away. Rich had a beautiful yard filled with all kinds of plants I didn't recognize. He also had a patch of black-eyed Susans. Before he moved, I asked him if I could take a few of those sunny yellow and brown flowers for our newly-established garden. He patiently explained how to dig them up and to make sure we made a deep and wide enough hole for them. We talked about sun and water requirements and how to make sure they flourished.

I think those were our first rescue plants. There are many different varieties of black-eyed Susans, just as there are many different dog breeds. And, like dogs, these joyful flowers are known for being highly adaptable and for surviving just about anywhere. They don't need exceptional soil, but they do need to be nurtured, just like dogs.

Rich's other neighbor was more of a bird and squirrel person than one who gardened. She had an abundance of birdseed containers throughout the front and back yard and all the woodland creatures hung out at her place. I guess my yard had zero appeal for animals. It was just a shortcut from point A to point B.

Two things happened one year that changed everything. Rich's neighbor Sarah moved away, taking her birdseed buffet leaving the chipmunks, bunnies, and squirrels to find other food sources. The second thing is that I began to care about my garden.

We decided to go native in our back yard and, while it was a ton of work, it does attract bees and butterflies galore. And then the fun began. Well, fun for Coconut, not for me.

I had visions of a colorful garden with tall plants waving in the breeze. What I had not counted on was the ever-increasing number of rodents. And bunnies. I learned that they taunt dogs.

As soon as the plants grew to the height where they provided cover, the rabbits and squirrels would lead my dog on a merry chase into the garden where he'd trample anything in his path. The rustling noise and downed branches and flowers had me pulling out a mental calculator as I accessed the financial damage and replacement costs of the murdered plants. Before I got too stressed, I figured out that what mattered were the roots. As long as they didn't get dug up the pretty parts would bloom the following year.

And then one morning, after I let Coconut out for his morning pee, he scampered back with his first kill. Okay, I exaggerate. His first stun. He dropped it on the sidewalk and looked at me all proud and sassy. The poor bunny was playing possum so that this wild beast would let him go.

His prey was terrified, Coconut was proud, I was horrified, and Gary, who relocated the poor bunny a couple of blocks away, was non-chalant. Of course, where there's one, there are others, and the garden dance continues. I've given up.

Chipmunks were the next unwanted discovery in my yard. I never saw a chipmunk until I moved to Wisconsin. I'm sure they were around when I was a kid growing up in Kansas, but I don't remember seeing them. It's probably because all we had was mud and dirt, which didn't provide any food for what I call "Satan's pets."

I truly thought that chipmunks were Disney fun-loving cartoon creations. I now hate chipmunks because they are destructive. They eat through building foundations and wires and they truly do torment my poor dog.

It seems that Coconut is an excellent barker and chaser, and we're down to one chipmunk. And every spring he still chases the poor guy all over my yard. I told the property management firm that Rich's house has holes in the foundation, and that's where the scared chipmunks hide. They didn't listen, so it's not my problem.

Something new is always happening in my yard, and it's not always good. I'm thinking it must have been a hawk that dropped a dead animal behind the Hostas bed. That decomposition smell with the side dish of maggots happened way too quickly to assume that Coconut actually killed something. Yes, clean up was as disgusting as you'd imagine. Dogs do not always digest stuff as quickly as you would think. Antibiotics are a miracle.

My first black-eyed Susans and Coconut are close in age, and they are both doing great. Like these cheerful wildflowers that last incredibly long, growing in garden beds, roadsides, and even in pavement cracks, Coconut is the perfect symbol of resilience, motivation, and encouragement.

Owning a dog is much more of a joy than I ever imagined it would be. Despite the garden trampling, rabbit stunning, and entrail eating, I would not give up Coconut for anything. But every day there's something to look forward to and enjoy. Just like in my garden.

OUR "PUREBRED POOCH"
Charlotte H. Burkholder

"No animal I know of can consistently be more of
a friend and companion than a dog."
— Stanley Leinwall

We said our goodbyes and cried our tears for our beloved Daisy. We never bothered to do a DNA test, because she was just our girl. Daisy resembled a border collie, and we had adopted her as an adorable puppy. Her shiny black coat and pure white chest made her easy to spot, and we loved her for thirteen years. She developed health issues, and even though it was one of the hardest things we'd ever done, she knew she was loved in those final moments.

Marlin and I agreed that we'd never own another dog. It wasn't just the goodbye part, which was one reason, but we were in our senior years with full lives. Plus, we knew we would never find a dog to equal Daisy.

Heidi, our veterinarian daughter, lived 100 miles away, and she thought no home should be without a dog. She kept her eyes open for possible pooches, and email notification sounds began alerting us to a parade of adoptable dogs.

One day she expressed an added urgency for us to reconsider. "Mom, you've got to come look at this dog!"

"This dog" turned out to be a black pup, approximately two years old. "Come visit us," Heidi invited. "We will take the dog home for the weekend, and you can see how you like him before saying no." Against our better judgment, we accepted her invitation.

If we ever did get a dog, even though we knew that wasn't even a remote possibility, he would have to meet our requirements: small lap dog, travels well, doesn't bark, calm, gentle. But we didn't want a dog.

On our way to see "this dog" for the first time, I chose a name for him. After all, I couldn't call him "this dog" for a whole weekend! I named him, 'Lil Daze in memory of Daisy.

Heidi works at a twenty-four-hour emergency clinic. One night the police had arrived, carrying a pitiful, injured, flea-infested, worm-bag of a dog. The pup had been hit by a vehicle. He refused to use one leg but had no broken bones. He must have struggled to keep himself alive. We could easily count his ribs.

After ten weeks at the clinic, he was healthy, free of fleas and worms, and had no sign of any of the previous leg weakness. He was ready for a loving home. Marlin and I were reluctantly willing to at least take a look at this dog.

We drove two hours to the veterinarian clinic. As we stood waiting for our first glimpse of him, butterflies flitted about in my stomach. The door opened. Out came a tail-wagging pup who welcomed our petting and cooing. 'Lil Daze nestled in my arms as I carried him to our car. On our way to Heidi's house, he threw up—more than once. One requirement failed! But he didn't bark, and he was small.

I fell in love with 'Lil Daze. The more I thought about it, the more I wanted to take him home. Unfortunately, Marlin didn't. He felt strongly that it would change our lifestyle too much. "Honey, you know we still travel a good bit, and there's always the problem of boarding."

But he reconsidered when he saw how much I wanted him.

'Lil Daze came home with us and settled right in. He didn't bark and had a calm, gentle manner. But he was hungry and gobbled up his meal, throwing it up after a few minutes. We tried different kinds of food. Still, he would eat as fast as he could and repeat the regurgitation.

Our local vet recommended that we put a medium-sized rock in his dish, forcing him to eat slower. This allowed his food to settle before he could rid himself of it. We figured he must have had to fight for his food all his young life to survive. "Gobble it fast, or it won't last," seemed to be his motto. The rock helped, and he soon learned that his food would not be snatched away if he took his time to eat.

He liked being on top of things. On his first night, he chose to sleep on a kitchen chair instead of the comfy, soft cushion-bed we'd made for him. Later in the day, we discovered him on top of our glass-top patio table. Stretched out in the sun, he made a beautiful picture of complete relaxation and peace. On the internet, we found he most resembled flat coat retrievers. His long silky ears, however, were definitely of the cocker breed. We call him our purebred pooch.

He became an excellent traveler after his eating habits improved. We could drive for hours and almost forget he was with us. He would lie on the back floor asleep, never making a sound. Later, he decided the seat might be preferable. Later yet, he decided he belonged up front.

When we left him in the car while we shopped, we would return to find him sitting behind the driver's wheel or in the passenger seat. Even after we deposited him in the back where he belonged, he scrambled up over the console and try to sit in my lap. Another failed requirement. He had grown way beyond lap dog size. But he didn't know that. He worked hard at fulfilling that requirement for us.

We learned, from the internet, that flat coat retrievers grow very slowly. The pup we brought home was now pushing thirty-five pounds. But he still thought he was a lap dog.

He made up for it with his personality. He loved people. He looked expectantly for a pat on the head or scratch behind the ears from the people he knew, as well as from strangers. When we moved from our home to a retirement community, he adjusted without a problem. Perfectly content as long as we were around, he made friends with everyone he met.

He earned the reputation of being the most beautiful and calm dog. Everybody's favorite, he received more treats than he should have, which is why the pounds kept inching up. But no one could resist those big, brown, pleading eyes.

Marlin and 'Lil Daze are best buddies. 'Lil Daze spends time in the woodworking shop with Martin, sleeping contentedly on an old pillow or watching the door for someone to come in who just might have a treat for him. We thought we had rescued 'Lil Daze, but as it turned out, 'Lil Daze has enriched our lives in countless ways. 'Lil Daze is family!

LIGHTBULB MOMENTS
Edwina Ditmore

"The love of a rescue dog is the most genuine and pure love you can find. They are living proof that love and trust can be renewed and rebuilt."
— Ashley Owen Hill

Before I started being a foster mom, I had many other dogs in my life. Schedules got crazy with work and family, and I ended up with an "oops litter" from Poochie and Cleo when I didn't get my dogs fixed quickly enough. Since then, I've made it a point to spay and neuter on schedule.

The entire litter got Egyptian names because my middle daughter was obsessed with all things Egypt at the time. We found homes for all but Tut, who ended up staying with us and was one of my best dogs ever. He was a little, shall we say, opinionated. He tolerated baby puppies, kind of, but he could not handle adult dogs coming into his territory. Tut was my crowd control and, while he had his quirks, as all dogs do, I loved him dearly.

Because Tut was okay with puppies, I started working with our local humane shelter. As a foster mom to newborn pups, I had to make sure they were fed every two hours each day. The other challenge was to help them poop, since this is something they can't do on their own. The third chore was giving them a bath multiple times a day.

I loved the puppies, but they usually get adopted more quickly because they are cute and cuddly. Too often, people overlook seniors because they might not be playful or exude cuteness.

There are all sorts of reasons why seniors end up homeless. They could have started life in a puppy mill and, when they became useless, they were kicked to the curb. Some have expensive health problems their owner could not afford. Still others wound up in kennels because their owners died. Whatever the reason, the thought of a senior dog with no one to love it tore me up inside. I decided that this was the age group I wanted to foster.

Several years after Tut passed, I knew it was time, and I started rescuing seniors. Over the years I have had many come and go. A few have become foster fails and end up living with me permanently. Some have crossed over the rainbow bridge. Others are still with me, and there will undoubtedly be more in my future.

I am every bit as much of a senior as those I foster. As I write this, I think of the dogs I currently foster or own and how we are going through the changes together. I currently have one that is in kidney failure and is deaf, one has congestive heart failure. Another short-term foster is blind in one eye and has no teeth.

Two of my dogs came to me from a hoarding situation. My area shelter called and asked if I could help foster a couple of the twelve dogs they rescued from a home where they'd found eighty dogs, mostly in one room. From what the shelter knew, they were never handled, none had been socialized, and they were all terribly frightened and feral.

By the time I was made aware of this situation, all but two of the dogs were in foster homes. They asked if I could help, and I didn't hesitate. I took Toby home and Bob went to another foster home.

Toby had no idea how to be a dog. He was paralyzed with fear. I had to start with the basics. He would not move out of his kennel if I was in the room. He would not eat in front of me. I could touch him, but that clearly terrified him.

Over time, Toby improved in small increments. We moved from being able to touch to petting and brushing. He wasn't crazy about the idea, but he allowed it.

I learned how to see the most miniscule change as great progress. He made eye contact. *Amazing!* He ate his food when he could still see me.

It's a miracle! He allowed me to put a collar on him. The list of tiny accomplishments went on and on.

He was always okay with the other dogs, probably because that's all he had ever known. Eventually, I started bringing him from his safe room into the living room, where I would sit and watch television with the other dogs. I would carry him in and settle him on my lap and, when it was time to go to bed, I'd carry him to his bed in another room. What a huge day it was when he chose to walk back by himself when he was ready.

I don't know what triggered the lightbulb moment, but one day he came out of his room on his own and jumped on the couch like a real dog! That was a huge milestone, and after that he came and went regularly.

Once he turned that corner, it was full speed ahead. He suddenly was going outside with the other dogs, playing with toys, and loving life. I always wished I could peek inside his head to see what changed.

He doesn't like anyone but me, and he will still get jumpy if something changes, but he is a million miles from where he started. We tried introducing him to potential adopters twice, but those homes didn't work out, so he became my third foster fail, and I have never regretted it.

We were settled in and I had no plans to take in more dogs at the time. But we all know about the best laid plans. I received an email from the shelter where I had gotten Toby, asking if I could possibly add another dog to our home. It seems that Bob, the dog rescued from the same hoarding situation as Toby, had been in a foster home, but he was not thriving. Of course, I said yes.

I quickly learned that Bobby, the name I started calling him, was not the same as Toby. Despite a year in a foster home, he was still terrified of everything. The biggest hurdle we faced, and still face, is that he is very afraid of being picked up. I had planned on following the same path with him that I had with Toby, but that wasn't going to work.

He has been with me for a few months now, and it is slow going. We have our victories and we have set backs. We go three steps forward, and two steps back. But I will not give up. A sweet, loving dog is somewhere in there, and I am determined to get him to see that as well.

Bobby has the capacity to love, as I believe all frightened dogs do. He just needs time, patience, and a never-ending amount of love.

We are back to the tiny steps stage. He lets me pet him and will even roll over for belly rubs. He loves all of my dogs, especially Toby. I was worried that after a year they wouldn't remember each other, but they clearly do.

I am confident that Bobby will have the lightbulb go on someday, just as Toby did.

As I write this, Toby is snoring in the bed beside my desk. My other dogs are all asleep without a care in the world. Bobby is in his room, sleeping and perhaps dreaming of better days ahead. I don't know what the future holds for any of my rescues. They each have challenges and their own paths to follow, but I do know it is my privilege and my joy to be a part of their journey.

SPOILED IN ALL THE RIGHT WAYS
Sandra Dennis

*"Saving one dog will not change the world, but surely
for that one dog, the world will change forever."*
— Karen Davison

My husband passed away from a brief, but grueling, battle with cancer in mid-2019. We had a houseful of Dalmatians our entire marriage and we lost our last one, fifteen-year-old Stella, during my husband's final days at home. It was a double whammy. An empty house, no husband, and no dogs. I retired at the end of that painful year and was looking forward to figuring out the next phase of my life.

I wasn't sure what it would look like, but I knew it would involve travel. My corporate job had required my going to many interesting cities around the globe, and I enjoyed those trips for the most part. But the freedom to see new places without the burden of work excited me. I decided that my first junket would be a long-awaited trip to Alaska with a friend.

We all know what happened in 2020, and travel was one of first things impacted. Then came restaurants, stores, churches, and gatherings of any sort. I'd always known a dog would be part of my life again, but, with no travel on the horizon, the time table had changed.

I'd been registered with Cavalier Rescue Midwest for a few months when along came Sadie. Sadie was a Blenheim (white and chestnut) Cavalier King Charles spaniel. These dogs were all fostered living in private homes until they were ready to be adopted.

Sadie's foster mom had sent me photos: Sadie in the garden, Sadie laying on the mat, Sadie cuddling with her foster brothers and sisters. She was absolutely adorable, but she came with some baggage.

Sadie was nearly seven when I adopted her. Her breeder had surrendered her when she was no longer an asset to their business. Poor Sadie, who had lived in a barn her entire life, had to learn how to be a dog and not a puppy-breeding machine.

People and life outside of a barn were new to her. She had been in foster care a little longer than usual because it was the pandemic and everyone was sheltering in place. Even though I only knew her from the photos and stories, I was already in love. I counted the weeks and days and then the hours until her gotcha day.

She finally came to live me in June. Our early days together were spent getting to know each other. At first, Sadie scooted away from me. I needed to earn her trust. We stood together outside in the mosquito-infested backyard as Sadie figured out her new potty routine.

Even though she was scared, Sadie stayed close by, my little shadow wherever I went. Private time in the bathroom was a thing of the past; Sadie followed me everywhere. She snuggled up close whenever I sat down and snored like a trucker when she slept—knowing she was finally in a comfortable, safe spot.

Thunderstorms and fireworks scared her; we snuggled even closer at those times. If puppy sounds were on the television, she'd lift her head, and you could see her wondering where those sweet babies were—I have a feeling she was a great mom. We went to visit friends, took trips to pet-friendly stores as things opened up, and went on lots of walks, which was good for both of us.

Sadie seemed to be a little more relaxed when other dogs were around—it's probably all she knew—so my grand puppy, Cosmo, came to visit often. It takes a lot to overcome seven years of life in a barn. When we couldn't be around people, we had each other. Once Sadie became a part of my family, it was hard to believe I'd been dog-less for even a few months.

Sadie and I have been together for three years. She's still a little shy, except when it comes to Phyllis down the street who always has a treat. Even though she knows my son, this girl still barks at him from time to time when he visits. New situations throw her for a loop. Thunderstorms still make her a little nervous and fireworks are evil.

While the seven years before I adopted Sadie were hard on her, I know she is living her best life, being spoiled in all the ways she deserves. Sadie loves her walks and when I brush her hair, which she adores, we gaze into each other's eyes, and I tell that her she's my best friend forever and that I know I'm her whole world.

I've learned quite a bit about this particular breed, and we have become a foster home for Cavalier Rescue Midwest. I say "we" because Sadie is great at tutoring the new barn dogs who are getting ready for their forever homes in all the good things in life. She shows them where the best rabbit smells are in the yard, how to catch popcorn when it's movie night, how to beg treats from the neighbors during walks and, especially, how to snuggle really close to your human every chance you get.

CHAPTER THREE

MILKWEED
HOPE

61

GRANDPA'S NOT JUST EIGHT

*"Every challenge, every adversity, contains within it
the seeds of opportunity and growth."*
—Roy Bennett

They may not have been the first three words I ever heard him speak, but I probably heard him say "You wanna shot?" over a thousand times. With that face-brightening grin, almost like the little boy who knows he got away with sweets from his mom's cookie jar, he'd ask that question of anyone who walked into the house.

When I married his son, I got a family like no other. The marriage didn't last, but my father-in-law never stopped caring. He embraced me whenever I visited, and we shared many interesting conversations. When I moved back to the Midwest with my new husband, he offered Gary a shot, and they settled down and talked like old friends.

I brought a shepherd's pie to a family Christmas party one year. After tasting it he asked me to go to the kitchen, get a container, and wrap the rest of it for him to take home. When I told him people were still going through the line and maybe they'd want some, he said they had plenty of other food to eat.

And so began our biannual trek from Wisconsin to Illinois, with shepherd's pie, quiche, soups, and banana bread. As Gary and Grandpa drank their shots, I put the food into the freezer for him to eat whenever he wanted. He chose to live alone and so giving him food to heat up was one tiny thing I could do for him.

He was of the same generation as Jimmy Carter, had a similar work ethic and kindness, and they were the same age. As my four-year-old grandson said after the last party celebrating his great-grandfather's birthday, "Grandma! Grandpa's not just eight. He's ninety-eight!"

Gracious, kind, intelligent, a great father, a wonderful grandfather, and a man of God and golf. If I had interviewed candidates to be my children's grandfather and my grandson's great-grandfather, I could not have found a better person.

I loved that he never stopped learning. Grandpa started raising monarch butterflies at his son's suggestion. For six or seven years he planted milkweed as they are the only food source for the monarch caterpillar larvae. He'd carefully search beneath the milkweed leaves and gently collect all the eggs he found. He delighted in watching each egg hatch into a caterpillar and transform into a chrysalis. I'm likely missing a few steps, but we were there a few years ago for the first flight.

We happened to arrive on the same day Grandpa was set to let the monarchs go. He raised them with such love and care, and then he gently set them onto the tree in the back yard and flashed his biggest grin as they flew away to live their new lives.

Grandpa kept a little log book that listed every butterfly he ever raised. After the monarchs were safely launched, he showed us his set up and talked about the process.

As is the case with all plants, the milkweed has more than one symbolic meaning, including hope. This outwardly humble plant's ability to transform from a weed to a source of nourishment for one of the world's most delicately beautiful and captivating creatures is infinitely hopeful.

To some people, rescue dogs are sort of the weeds of the canine population. Maybe they need a good grooming or they have some health or behavioral issues. Guess what happens when they find the right home? I find hope in their resilience and their willingness to be like that butterfly—knowing their job, doing it well, and adding so much to their families and our world.

We knew this would be our last visit before Grandpa left the body that he no longer needed and flew to heaven. In between Gary's first and second knee replacement surgery last year we had a break in the weather so we could drive down to see Grandpa.

He wasn't a dog person, but we took Coconut with us. People came to visit Grandpa and share stories—and, through it all, there was Coconut.

Grandpa didn't talk much—he rambled and dozed off—but Coconut seemed to know not to jump on this frail man. At one point Grandpa awoke and his blue-veined, papery thin hand stroked Coconut's soft fur. When his hand fell limp, my dog found the patch of sun near Grandpa's feet, content to be in a room full of love and conversation.

I'm glad we took Coconut on that goodbye journey. I'd like to think that the man who was not a dog person took comfort in him. I hope everyone who needs one can have a dog; even those who don't know it yet.

I will never make shepherd's pie without a sense of loss. But this year, when the monarchs come to visit our rain garden, I will remember this extraordinary man who made the world a better place.

HOPE ISN'T ALWAYS NOISY
Don Hughes

"Rescue dogs are not damaged or broken. They have been tested, and they come out stronger. They have proven that nothing can break their spirit."
— Sharon Ann Myers

As I entered the Maricopa County Animal Care and Control West Shelter, I felt a mix of excitement and anxiety. I had walked through those blue double doors hundreds of times in the previous three years as a weekend volunteer. But today was different. Today, I wasn't reporting for duty.

Today, I was coming to meet Barbie.

A few nights earlier, Andrea, another volunteer friend, had posted a video of Barbie on Facebook. I first noticed her tawny color, black muzzle, and four white socks. Her tail curled up with a white tip, like it had been dipped in vanilla ice cream, and her head was topped by big, black-tipped ears that would occasionally fold in half. In the video, she was visibly shaking. I could see the fear in her eyes, even though she never looked directly into the camera. She appeared skinny and slightly malnourished. *She's so scared and sad*, I thought as I watched. *I have to meet her.*

I had seen a lot of scared dogs at the shelter. Every dog had a hard luck story—from abused dogs to the ones surrendered by their owners. I should have become hardened to these sad cases; instead, these stories motivated me to keep coming back, to do what I could to help. Maybe I could work to help her become adoptable as I had other project dogs. Still, everything felt different for some reason. Maybe it was her sad eyes. As I continued walking past the reception area, I reminded myself I traveled too much to have a dog.

Barbie had been picked up as a stray. Her three months at the shelter had not gone well. Each week she deteriorated even more. Staff and volunteers had tried to work with her, but she was afraid of men. That was the first of many red flags. Could she overcome her fear of men, specifically me? Did I have what it took to help her?

As I walked into Building A, the noise level increased significantly. Barbie's kennel was towards the back of the building. As I passed the forty or fifty dogs barking excitedly, I saw hope in their begging eyes. Hope that maybe this human would be take them away from this scary place and give them the family they desperately needed. Some people were turned off by the barking and jumping, but I chose to see the dogs as lost souls reaching out into the darkness, hoping someone would stop and see what a beautiful dog sat behind the wire gate. One thing I learned is that hope can be noisy.

Not all the dogs were noisy and excited. Some were shy, scared, and forlorn souls—the ones who had simply given up. Since they weren't barking or jumping, people would just keep walking.

Barbie was one of those dogs. Alone, curled in a tight ball in the farthest corner of her kennel, hoping no one would notice her. But I did. She was so skinny I could see the outline of her spine and rib cage.

The stress of being in the shelter for so long was preventing her from gaining weight. According to her notes, she was three or four years old. The shelter staff thought she was a shallow collie, meaning she had short hair, unlike Lassie's long fur.

I crawled past the dog poop into the back of her kennel and put my leash on her. Reluctantly, she followed me out of her kennel. She didn't bolt or pull like other rescue dogs. She walked well enough on the leash, but there was no clue if she was happy or sad.

After a jaunt around the yard, I took Barbie into a meet-and-greet room to see how scared she was. Once inside, Barbie immediately curled into a tight bunch, trying to become invisible. She made no eye contact, and while she didn't recoil from my touch, it was clear she didn't like it. She didn't show much interest in me either. All of these things should have been warning signs. For me however, after being a volunteer and seeing all sorts of dogs, it was validation that Barbie needed someone to believe in her enough to try to work with her.

When I looked into her eyes, I saw no hope, no spark, just despair. Driving home I couldn't stop thinking about Barbie, wondering if this time, I had found the dog to take home. Still unsure, my resolve to help this sad dog was strong.

I went back to see Barbie a second time and took her home for a day foster. She showed no recognition nor was there any interaction between us. I had never taken care of a dog before. I wasn't sure that I was up for the challenge of caring for an animal with behavioral problems.

I let the staff know that if they found an adopter or a foster, that was fine, but to call me before she was put on the euthanasia list. Sadly, Barbie deteriorated further in her kennel. She was scheduled to be put down in three days. I had no time for waffling or agonizing. Either I adopt Barbie, or she would die on Monday.

After a long night of soul searching, I decided to adopt Barbie, I just could not let her die. Sometimes, you just have to have faith that everything will work out and jump in head first.

Her deterioration the week after our day foster was worse than I imagined. She refused to walk on the leash or jump in the car. Barbie was just shaking from fear. But she wasn't shaking when I brought her home. I took that as a small positive step. Barbie almost fell asleep standing up; she was just too scared to lie down.

I knew this would be difficult, but I wasn't prepared for just how big of a challenge it would be. Barbie needed someone she could believe in and trust. That would be me—she just didn't know it yet.

The first three months were difficult. For every step forward, we took two or more steps back. Walks, food, structure, and patience would be my approach to gaining Barbie's trust. I needed that if the great dog hidden behind all of her fear was ever going to appear. Given how badly the first day had gone, I wasn't sure this was going to work. But if I failed, I knew the alternative was a return to the shelter and the inevitable.

Barbie likely had never been inside a house before. Three months at the shelter with no training meant no house training, and that proved to be a major challenge.

In her past, it didn't matter where or when she went to the bathroom. Now it did. She simply didn't know what I wanted from her, and I didn't know how to teach her.

Slowly, our communication skills began to improve. I become more aware of her signals when she needed to go outside. If I was working in my office and she came in and lay down, that meant everything was fine. When Barbie came in and stared at me, or put her paw on me, she wasn't being cute. She was telling me, "I've got to go now."

As her confidence and trust grew, we began exploring more of our neighborhood and surrounding parks. For me, walks were no longer mere exercise; they were an adventure, as I began to see the world through her eyes.

Soon I noticed that one of Barbie's walking goals was ensuring that we were saved from any terrorists masquerading as a rabbit or lizard. Often, after our junkets, Barbie would race around the house, past the dining room table, and leap over the couch again and again until she was breathing heavy. I would then tell her to lay down on the coach. The look on her face was pure joy, as if she had had more fun than any dog ever had.

Now when she lies down next to me, she rests her head or paw on my leg or arm, whichever is closer. At times she looks up at me with those big, brown eyes, and I know all is right with the world. Sometimes I wonder what I did to deserve a love such as this. We still need to work on some things, but I know the love and trust we've built through trial and error will get us through whatever life wants to throw at us.

FILLING AN EMPTY NEST
Leola R. Ogle

"A dog doesn't care if you're rich or poor, smart or dumb.
Give him your heart . . . and he'll give you his."
— Milo Gathema

We had few pets during my childhood or when my children were grow-ing up. Pets were for people who could afford to feed and take care of them. Or, if you lived in lived in rural area where animals could fend for themselves, then maybe you'd have a dog or a cat. We didn't fit either of those descriptions.

We had a few pets when my children were young, but I wasn't attached to any of them. I was raising five children while trying to survive in a bad marriage. A pet was just one more thing I had to worry about.

With only two teenage daughters left at home, I went through a tough divorce. A few years later, I remarried. Jeff had spent his childhood in rural areas and always had pets of every kind. When we moved from our condo and bought a home, Jeff and his two sons wanted a dog.

Comet was a basset hound who, sadly, didn't work out in a house-hold as busy as ours. Everyone was gone a lot, and Comet grieved at being alone. We gave her to our daughter and her husband who had Bella, Comet's sister. Comet thrived there.

Soon after my grandson Jonathan moved in with us, he found a Labrador/mix puppy abandoned by a busy highway on a Sunday night after church. You would think with three teenage boys in our home, they could take care of one puppy, but the task fell to me. And I was soon in love with the gentle girl we named Abigail.

Then one blistering, Arizona, summer day my sweet girl passed away from a stroke after a series of seizures. Abigail was the first pet I can say I truly loved, and I could not bring myself to go to the vet with Jeff. I know I should have been there, and to this day I regret the choice I made, but sometimes watching a loved pet fade away is more than a heart can handle, and so we paid our vet to take care of her remains.

Abigail was closest to me, and her passing hurt more than I imagined it would. My being a senior seemed to make it worse. Maybe I was questioning my own mortality, but I missed her terribly. I had experienced multiple crises and hardships in my life, so the depth of my grief surprised me. Heartsick, I told my husband, "No more dogs. I can't go through this again."

Weeks passed, then months. Like the seasons, our lives had changed. We became empty nesters. At first it was glorious, but then I felt restless. I had been birthing and raising babies and kids since I was sixteen. Although I saw my children, grandchildren, and great-grandchildren weekly, something was lacking in my life

After a year, for my birthday in July, I told Jeff I was ready for another dog. And I prayed a simple prayer: "Lead us to a good dog, Lord, the one we're meant to have."

We had rescued Abigail from the streets and I knew I wanted another rescue dog. We weren't in a hurry, so it wasn't until one October day nine years ago that my husband found our next dog. He had arrived early at a job site, and with time to kill, he wandered into a nearby pet rescue adoption event.

He came home with Ravioli, a white Jack Russell terrier/Chihuahua/ mix with black spots. The pet store workers had given the feisty two-year-old the silly name, and we decided a new moniker was in order. We changed my birthday dog's name to Bucky after Captain America's friend, Buchanan, because my husband is a Marvel super-hero fan.

Jeff and I quickly bonded with this small whirlwind of attitude and personality. We quickly realized how smart Bucky was and how to adapt to his quirks.

As smitten as I was with our new dog, it soon became obvious that Bucky was more Jeff's dog than mine. My dear husband was going through an emotionally trying time, and Bucky sensed it. I was amazed to watch my husband's depression dissipate as he interacted with this dog. I was experiencing firsthand what many others have always known—our pets can bring more than joy and comfort to our lives; they can bring healing.

I obviously hadn't understood how therapeutic it would've been for Jeff if I had greeted him at the door every day with a squeaky toy in my mouth while I jumped on his legs and pranced in circles around him. Jeff's laughter at Bucky's antics was music to my ears.

I was the woman who swore she would never dish out money for a large vet bill because they were just animals. Unfortunately, Bucky's little-dog-with a-big-dog-attitude got him seriously injured a couple of times during our evening walks. Although we always kept Bucky on a leash, twice he started fights with large dogs running loose in our neighborhood. How things change when you fall in love with the right dog. I sat in a waiting room with Jeff holding our injured dog while I cried and prayed.

Time marched on, and Bucky became old, fat, and grumpy. My husband and I had no desire for a second dog. But as Bucky's health began to decline, I wondered what I would do when Bucky passed.

One day while I scrolling on Facebook, I saw a picture of Milo. Milo had been living on the streets until he was lured into captivity by offerings of food. After a couple of weeks of caring for Milo, my friend sent out a plea to find a loving home for the pup.

I showed his picture to Jeff. "He's sure good looking, huh? What do you think?"

The vet aged him between one year and eighteen months. After we adopted him, we had his DNA tested and learned that his dominate breeds include rottweiler, pug, and chow chow.

Bonding wasn't easy at first because to Milo, Jeff represented vet shots, neutering, and wearing a cone. Milo bonded with me weeks before he would even stay in the same room with Jeff. In the beginning, Jeff dubbed Milo "ninja" and "ghost" for his stealth in slipping past us unnoticed.

Bucky was not thrilled about sharing his humans with another pooch after nine years of being the only dog. Milo was almost feral, and it was interesting to watch Bucky assert his alpha male dominance over the bigger, stronger, second dog while Milo adjusted to his place in our family.

It only took a few months, and now our happy three-year-old rarely hides under our bed, is affectionate and playful, and challenges Bucky on occasion for alpha dominance.

We are no longer empty nesters and our patched-together family of four is perfect for us.

LOVE LIKE BLACKBERRIES
Brenda Kay Ledford

"I am among the ranks of millions of people who
appreciate the souls of dogs and know they are a gift
of pure love and an example of all that is good."
— Jennifer Skiff

I decided it was time to adopt a dog so I went to Valley River Humane Society in Marble, North Carolina. I strolled into the shelter and covered my ears as the dogs howled. The animals leapt and scratched at their cages as I walked past them. Their sad eyes begged for attention. I jerked when a wolf dog stood and towered like a colt. I wanted to take them all home. Even that wolf dog.

And then I saw him, dark as black pepper and lying in the corner. He looked up at me with those inky eyes, and still he did not bark. Instead, when I neared his cage, he stuck his paw through the wire and shook hands like a politician. Then he perked up his triangle-shaped ears and licked my face. My heart melted.

"Do you want to go home with me?" I asked and stroked his side.

Pepper whined and lounged against the pen. He wanted to bust out of this place now. Of course, I could not take him home until I filled out the papers and a vet neutered him. I gave the information to the shelter manager and then zipped back to tell Pepper good-bye.

He howled when I started out the door.

"I'll get you on Friday at the vet's office. Don't cry, Pepper. I promise I will bring you to your forever home."

A chorus of barks echoed in the shelter. But not my dog. He sat and watched me leave, probably wondering why he wasn't coming along.

On Friday, Mama and I arrived early at the veterinarians' office. Pepper marched beside the vet and rushed to greet me. "He knows you," said Dr. Cranford.

I smiled like a proud parent and took Pepper's leash. He pulled me down the hall, bounded down the steps, and fairly galloped across the parking lot. There was no doubt Pepper wanted to go home with me.

We've had many adventures since he came to live with me. Today was one I knew he would enjoy, because Pepper loves blackberries and, in moderation, they are a healthy treat.

The early morning golden light bathed the Blue Ridge Mountains, and the sun hung like a ruby over the ridgeline. Spiderwebs draped blades of grass like a silver shawl as peaches plopped to the ground. A chilled breeze carried the scent of honeysuckle to where Pepper curled up like a carpet of black velvet.

I opened his gate, and he sprang into action, as he does every morning. "Yelp! Yelp! Yelp!" He jumped to my shoulders leaving a trail of paw prints my T-shirt.

"Stop, Pepper!"

He thumped his tail, twirled around like a top, then lunged and washed my face with dog kisses.

"Yuck! If I had wanted a bath . . ."

The black Labrador retriever whined and tucked his tail between his legs. "It's okay, Pepper. I know you're just happy to see me."

"Woof! Woof!" he barked and kissed my hands.

How could I stay angry with this adorable, beautiful animal? He's my child, dependent upon me for his care. All he needs is love. Even my mama says that Pepper will make a fine dog. Sure, he's hyperactive, but Pepper is only two-years-old. He will settle down soon.

"You wanna go berry picking?"

"Yap!" Yap!" he answered and sprang into the air.

We took off, and Pepper's tail twirled like a helicopter. He wiggled his rear end and explored the berry patch. I plucked berries and plopped them into the pail. He nudged my elbow and licked my arm. He whined, and I offered him a piece of fruit. He smacked his lips and gobbled a few of the black jewels. He helped me pick blackberries, and we took a bucket home to make jam.

In the evening, we rested on the front porch. Pepper put his chin on my lap. I stroked his silky head, and he washed my hands with his tongue. Pink plumes unfurled across the Shewbird Mountain as fireflies flickered beneath a canopy of stars. Pepper went to sleep at my feet, and my heart was filled with the joy that comes with having a best friend who loves me and blackberries.

THE HAPPIEST ENDING EVER
Karlene Leatherman

"The truth is that it's just really hard for me to get to sleep
without a dog in my bedroom."
— Jimmy Stewart

Many second-dog stories start with the death of a beloved pet, and that's how our story begins. We adopted Rudy in 2010 from the Oshkosh Area Humane Society when he was still a puppy. Dr. Heidi at the Animal Hospital told us he was a lemon beagle, a type of dog I'd never heard of. It didn't really matter about his breed, because he ended up being perfect for us.

Rudy was part of our family for almost thirteen years until he suffered a series of seizures one night. Nothing could help the quality of his life, so we decided to let him go.

I work part time and am active in our Rotary group, which means my husband, Dennis, is home alone quite a bit of the time. He had surgery scheduled, but, due to some complications, the procedure was postponed.

"Well, if the surgery isn't going to happen, then it's time to look for a dog," decreed Dennis. I wasn't sure about the timing, but Dennis was adamant, and it was January, the month of new beginnings.

We knew the surgery would likely be rescheduled, but by then, we hoped the new four-legged companion would be potty trained and settled in. We started our search online, found a dog we thought was a good match, and off we went to the shelter. As soon as we told the adoption counselor the dog's name, she explained that they already had several applications for him, and we should probably look at other pups.

I knew whoever we adopted was technically going to be for Dennis, but that I'd be responsible for much of his care. I didn't want a large or older dog. Our adoption counselor suggested we consider Winnie, a black, smooth-coat Chihuahua who was being fostered by a local family.

Winnie's previous owner had needed to make a decision after Winnie chewed the hand off a toy and got a bowel obstruction. The owner couldn't afford the surgery, so she had surrendered the dog to the same shelter where we'd adopted Rudy more than a decade earlier.

The shelter took on the financial cost of the life-saving surgery and set Winnie up with a foster family while she convalesced. When Winnie was approved for adoption, her foster dad brought her to the shelter to meet us. I'd never had the challenge of a shy dog, and Winnie was quite timid. We lured her to us with chicken which, as it turns out, she loves.

Besides being pretty and quiet, she was the right size and age, and so we completed the paperwork. A week later we took our new girl home. Besides the toy disaster, we didn't know much about her.

We quickly learned that she was either not potty trained or we hadn't figured out her signals. We quickly learned how to communicate with her, though, from time to time, she still has accidents in the house.

Since Winnie isn't very tall, we had to clear a path in the snow for her. Once the snow was gone, she loved having a large yard to explore. Winnie gets the zoomies and having a fenced yard is helpful.

Winnie tries her darndest to strike up a conversation with the big dog on the other side of the fence, but, so far, it's one-sided. Winnie's distinctive barks are met with silence, and that's the only time we ever hear her bark.

Now that she's over her shyness, Winnie is proving to be a championship lap dog. She might be Dennis' dog, but she makes sure to give me equal lap time. When she is not relaxing, this black beauty loves playing with toys.

Her foster parents sent her with a stuffed lamb, which she loved. She was relentless about tearing it apart. Seeing the joy that lamb brought to her, we bought some spares and hid them so that Winnie is never without her lambie.

I have to admit that Dennis was right when he said he needed a dog, and we both adore Winnie. She has a day bed in the front window that gets a lot of sun, and at night, she shares our bed.

We are both grateful for the surgery that Winnie received and the foster family that took care of her while she recuperated. Rescuing and rehoming dogs is a lot of work. Without foster families, many stories would have a different ending. We think our story has the happiest ending ever.

THE HEART STEALER
By Carla Stewart

"A puppy is so eager to please, it breaks your heart."
— Robert Falcon Scott

"No, we're not getting another dog."

That was my standard reply to anyone who asked, after we lost Zelda, our little red miniature Dachshund. For sixteen years, she'd been the love of our lives, adored by our grandchildren and all who knew her, my chair companion and muse as I'd written six novels. I couldn't imagine life without her. As her health began to fail, I clung to every memory and cuddled her more than ever.

When the pandemic came, I welcomed the opportunity to stay home all the time to be with Zelda. She slept in a doggie bed at my feet as I organized closets and photo albums, worked jigsaw puzzles, and worried. I cried every day when I thought of losing her. When would I know it was time to end her suffering?

By June of that confining time, I knew we'd be saying good-bye soon. On the day I scheduled to take her in, she had a neurological incident that caused intense pain. It confirmed my decision, but did little to comfort me. I cradled her in my arms until time for my husband, Max, to drive us to the vet.

Saying good-bye was even harder than I expected, and I vowed I would never have another dog. It hurt too much.

Life was empty without Zelda and even emptier when I lost my dad three months later. As the pandemic raged on, something in me shifted. I had no desire to continue work on my current novel. I turned to reading, but often a few pages in, my interest waned. COVID–19 meant that we didn't have any large holiday gatherings that year, and we saw family members rarely.

Slowly, the world began to open up, the vaccine came, and we took a couple of short trips, but my desire to return to my old pursuits dwindled even more. I spent most of my days on the patio watching the birds and daydreaming. Occasionally, as I read the newspaper, my eyes drifted to the want ads, specifically the pet section. I scrolled through puppy sites on the computer. The price of puppies had sky-rocketed since we'd gotten Zelda. And I really didn't want another dog, did I?

When airline travel resumed, we made a long-overdue trip to see our son and his wife in California. The chorus of their six dogs barking met us. Dog lovers extraordinaire, our kids' pups had come to them in a variety of ways. Two rescues, three purchased as puppies, and one sweet little cream-colored Chihuahua named Buddy, who belonged to Brett's mother-in-law. All of the dogs were friendly and affectionate, but Buddy waited patiently for the cue to jump on our laps. He would snuggle close, content with a tummy rub. The guard I'd built around my heart began to melt.

The next few months, we talked off and on about, not if we wanted another dog, but when. We planned a big trip for the fall of 2022, but a couple of weeks before we left, a lady with a local rescue posted online that she'd taken in a pregnant Chihuahua/mix who had now delivered four puppies. We tucked away the possibility of looking into it when our travels were over.

When we returned, new pics of the puppies popped up. One female in particular caught my eye: a tiny white curled-up ball with soft brown around the eyes and floppy brown ears.

Fast forward: paperwork, screening, meet and greet. Oh my good-ness, the one we'd chosen fit in my cupped hands, shivering, smaller than I expected. She had a round spot on her back the color of a new copper penny. I stroked her gently and whispered to her while Max pet-ted her mama. By the end of the visit, we agreed to adopt her.

The next few days were a whirlwind of puppy shopping. Pens, crate, soft toys, squeaky toys, doggie beds, puppy food, and dishes all found their way into our shopping cart in a way that reminded me of when we were expecting our first two-legged child. A light-hearted feeling crept over me.

Penny. It went with the spot on her back, but she needed another name. She was feisty and bounced in the grass like a toaster pastry. So, that's who she is. Penny PopTart.

The name fit her. As a matter of fact, her initial feistiness was more than we bargained for. Much more. She demanded constant attention. Chewing. Nipping. Middle of the night potty breaks. Bags developed under my eyes from exhaustion. Hopping up and down dozens of times a day to find Penny, take her out, play with her.

Honestly, at times I considered returning her to the rescue lady. But in the next moment, Penny would cock her head, those cute ears bent at the tips. Round chocolate-colored eyes shone with adoration, her complete and utter trust in me dissolving all thoughts of giving her up. The three of us—Max, Penny PopTart, and I— would get through this together somehow.

The holidays came, and this year, a house full of kids and grandkids tumbled on the floor with Penny, playing, loving on her, and laughing at her puppy kisses. My earlier thoughts of returning her evaporated. She was adored and loved, like Zelda before her. And yet, different from Zelda.

Zelda had been a much calmer lap dog. Both pups had gotten us out of the house, taking walks, meeting neighbors, playing fetch in the yard. Zelda, though, hadn't traveled well because of motion sickness. I had hated leaving her at the kennel, so we were delighted when Penny did well on her first car trip. She was a champion traveler the next time, too, and loved hotel rooms, meeting new people, and exploring her surroundings. The sort of things I love, too.

We're still learning each other's ways, and Penny is responding well to obedience training. Her energy is contagious, and lately I feel more like myself. The sense of purpose has returned. I'm writing some again—not the novel I was working on, but family stories. And you can be sure that Penny, our newest family member, will be in them.

Inquisitive. Smart. Sweet. And a petty thief. Our girl steals gloves from Max's pockets and tissues from mine. But most of all, she's stolen our hearts. She makes us furious at times, but she also makes us laugh every single day. Now I cannot imagine life without Penny PopTart.

THE JOY OF BEING MERRY
Gail Westrup

"Turning a troubled person's life around is difficult,
but rescuers with commitment and time, and a few dollars
can radically alter the fate of a dog."
— Jon Katz

Merry was a beautiful shade of red with white markings on her chest and paws.

An article in the weekly volunteer newsletter pegged her at "between two to three years old and terrified." That's the word their writer used. The person could easily have said, skittish, spooked, and distressed, because she was all those and then some.

Fourteen dogs had been captured after escaping from a hoarding situation during the holiday season. Merry, a mixed breed who looks like a small golden retriever, had been named by the volunteers involved in getting her to safety. Merry was the only one of the canine escapees who had ended up at the rescue where Doug and I volunteer.

We are retired empty-nesters, and at that time our nest was also minus any pets. We decided to foster Merry and give her a quiet place to begin anew away from the busy rescue facility.

After six months of love, patience, and even a class for shy dogs, Merry had become less fearful and more social. She was still shy; not at all like the outgoing goldens we'd previously owned. Week by week her tail wagging increased, as her fears about the world around her decreased.

She also became part of our family; we officially adopted her. We could have changed her name, but to us Merry was more than a name.

It was a statement of faith that someday this beautiful dog would experience the meaning of her name: Merry would be merry.

Doug and I love taking trips in our RV, and the three of us set off on a short trip in the Sierra Nevadas. The early summer weather was perfect, daytime highs in the seventies and evenings only dipping into the forties. The greenery and wildflowers were still on display, and, unless you're spending your time searching for a runaway dog, it's a great vacation spot.

We still aren't sure what prompted her sudden dash out of the RV that Saturday afternoon before we got her leashed, as was our habit. We did know that her history made getting her back a tough assignment.

Panicked and wide-eyed, I frantically ran though the RV resort chasing our dog. She was young, healthy, scared, and in her own world of panic. I'm fit for a woman in my 60s, but the race was way above my pay grade. She soon disappeared into the trees and shrubbery of the Sierra Nevada Mountains. I returned to our RV site breathless and nearly in tears as I told my husband and our travel companions that our dog was gone.

Shortly after my return to camp, we received our first clue to Merry's whereabouts. Relatives joining us for dinner had seen a loose dog they thought resembled Merry heading to the park entrance as they arrived. This was both good and bad news. The good part was because we had a starting point for our search. Sadly, it meant that she was running towards a busy road.

Instead of celebrating Doug's birthday as planned, we all spent the next few hours in separate vehicles driving the main roads looking for Merry. As the sun set with no sign of her, we returned to the RV to reheat dinner and discuss our strategy.

That night, after everyone left, I texted friends at home to ask for prayer. They were Merry's friends, too, as they had met and helped socialize her when she had first come to stay with us. As I sat outdoors asking God for help, I heard a familiar jingle: Merry's dog tags. I looked towards the sound and saw a pair of eyes.

Not wanting to startle her, I softly called her name. But she turned and ran, leaving me in tears. I was thankful that she was alive and nearby, but too aware that she was still out at night among coyotes and other wildlife. I knew I would face a long and sleepless night.

The next day, our fellow dog-loving RV travelers helped put up signs with a photo of Merry and my phone number. We got calls about sightings, but by the time we got there, she was gone. We sought advice from rescue organizations and the local animal control.

Our friends reached out to a woman they knew who helped find lost pets. While she couldn't travel to help us, she understood what we were going through. She agreed to loan us two live animal cage traps that would allow us to lure Merry in with food and catch her.

By Merry was so scared she was not going to come to anyone. Doug made the three-hour drive to borrow the traps and learn to use them. I stayed at the RV on the long shot that our prodigal dog would return. If someone was able to catch her, Merry needed to see her mom. I held onto the hope that this would happen that day. Unfortunately, the day ended with Merry still outdoors and me facing another night of very little sleep.

Doug slept at our home after his long day on the road and returned with two traps early the next morning. We had to work with the RV park managers regarding how and where we could set them up to ensure no other animals were accidentally caught. They also wouldn't allow us to leave them up after dark. We did our best, but the sun again set with our scared dog out in the wild.

During the following day, three scary nights, and two brutal days into our efforts, we discovered Merry seemed to be spending most of her time in the tall grass around a small pond. The RV Park gave us the okay to set up our trap in that area, provided we stayed close and kept watch. We used strong-smelling food to lure her in—and our dirty socks so she'd recognize our scent. Her favorite blanket was also there awaiting her return.

Doug set up the trap and parked his truck a short distance away, using binoculars to watch the pond area. We were all praying this would be the day Merry returned home. And it was.

Doug heard the trap close and a few yips letting us know that our girl was safe. As he approached, her face was startled, but her tail was wagging. Our scared little pup was back, tired and hungry, but otherwise fine.

That was a year and a half ago, and if you're wondering if Merry still travels with us the answer is yes. In the once-bitten-twice-shy category, she wears a GPS tracking device just in case. As an extra protective measure, we make sure she is leashed anytime the RV door is opened.

Merry loves her time with us, loves the outdoors, and especially loves the beach. To see her on her thirty-foot lead running zoomies in the sand or chasing seagulls, you'd never know this is the same terrified dog that ran from us for three days in the mountains. Our beautiful girl, head high and tail wagging, overcame the fears of her past and everyday experiences the joy of being Merry.

CHAPTER FOUR

SUNFLOWER LOYALTY

SUNFLOWER DOGS

"The poor dog, in life the firmest friend.
The first to welcome, foremost to defend."
– Lord Byron

When you are from a large family, you all have slightly different memories of the ways things happened when you were growing up. It's interesting at family gatherings to hear a sibling tell a story about an event that you know happened in a totally different way.

And then there's that one sibling who doesn't remember anything. After one too many times of my older brother Eric saying, "I don't remember that," I began to question whether he was even a part of our family.

But if I ask all my brothers and sisters what they remember about my sister Patricia, they would all say that she loved to chew gum and ate sunflower seeds. Some days I think she lived on those seeds. She was a world champion sheller, eater, and spitter-out-the-sheller while a spectator at an endless string of Daddy's summer softball games.

I was born and raised in Kansas, the state that designated the wild native sunflower as their official flower and floral emblem in 1903. The sunflower is also featured on the Kansas quarter, flag, and their nickname is, of course, "The Sunflower State." Even though I grew up there, I don't remember seeing fields of them until I went to Spain and we drove past miles and miles of these happy plants.

I did a lot of gardening last year. And the year before. You're probably sick of hearing me say this, but I do not particularly enjoy gardening. I do, however, enjoy the results. Except for my sunflowers.

I've tried to grow sunflowers from seed several years in a row and, no matter where I put them, I have not had success. They seem to be an effortless plant for everyone else in my neighborhood. When Coconut and I walk we see yards full of them. We've even gone to sunflower festivals and seen field after field like I saw in Spain.

Last year I decided to focus on adding more varieties of black-eyed Susans instead of sunflowers. One day I was out weeding, a never-ending task, and saw that a bird gifted me with a sunflower. Right in the most unwelcoming space in the entire yard next to the brick wall on the east side of my house. It's filled with rocks and weeds, and because of where it's situated, it doesn't get nearly the sun as everywhere else.

Week after week it grew taller with a massive stem, just about reaching the second story. I never watered it, didn't try to make the area nicer, and yet it flourished. Kind of like the pups I met at the rescue shelter over the years.

Strays, breeders, and abandoned dogs all have the ability to not only thrive but to bring us joy. Mythology tells us that sunflowers are a symbol of loyalty, endurance, and adoration. If that doesn't sum up a dog, I don't know what does. Little by little, just like my garden, these dogs began to grow into the dogs we knew they could be.

That sunflower planted in such an inhospitable place reminds me that dogs don't need fancy homes or extravagant toys and clothes. The need the nutrition, water, and love. They need training and vet care. What they give us in return is so much more than we should expect.

And, yes, Patricia still loves those seeds. Maybe when we visit a sunflower farm next time, I'll buy some seeds and eat them. I can promise you I'll be thinking about sitting on a hard bench looking at the ground covered with shells while I watched my dad play softball. And my sunflower dog will be next to me.

A TRICOLOR BALL OF ENERGY
Debra Mahoney

"When I look into the eyes of an animal, I do not see an animal.
I see a living being. I see a friend. I feel a soul."
— A.D. Williams

Life didn't turn out the way I had planned. I wasn't supposed to be divorced and living alone on a fixed income. I have a wonderful church, a group of friends I enjoy, and one of my daughters and her family lives in my town. But something was still missing in my life.

The idea of getting a dog wasn't a new thought. In fact, several friends suggested a canine companion would help in many ways. I would have someone to love me unconditionally, who would be there for me whenever I wanted. The idea of having someone to go with on long walks, and to share my life with seemed like a wonderful idea.

A friend worked with an independent rescue shelter that rescued dogs from a high-kill shelter in Kentucky. One of the things she did for them was to write the biographies, and she had advance knowledge of when dogs arrived that might be a good fit.

Now and then she'd alert me to a certain dog I should see. There were so many! It was hard to know how to choose. I also wondered about my ability to afford a dog because I'd had pets in the past and remembered the costs. I went back and forth for nine months, weighing the pros and cons of adopting a dog.

And then COVID-19 hit. When everything shut down it was devastating. I am a very social person, and being alone in my little apartment was getting harder. I knew that social media was simply not enough to see me through however long it was going to take for things to return to normal.

About two weeks after Christmas of 2020, my friend told me to go to the rescue's website. They had just received some adorable dogs who were under the twenty-five-pound weight limit my senior living community allowed.

The owner escorted us into one of the visiting rooms and brought out a two-and-a-half-month-old ball of energy. I was used to owning larger dogs, but one look at this little guy's tricolor face was all it took for me to fall in love. I gazed into those brown eyes, and I knew that this was the dog I had been looking for all of those months.

Many people thought I was crazy to adopt a puppy at my age. And when they learned he was a Jack Russell/beagle mix they weren't at all shy about voicing their opinions. He would be too high energy, he'd bark too much, and he wasn't potty trained were just a few of the reasons people said he was not the dog for me. All of those things were true, but it didn't matter. I knew this was my boy and that I was meant to be his mom.

There was such a rush to get puppies during this time that I had to decide right then. I can be indecisive when it comes to making life-changing decisions; this wasn't one of those times. I knew that he was going to add something I needed in my life that money could not buy.

The owner was nice enough to keep him for a week so that I could buy a kennel and other supplies. I gave my new puppy a hug, but he squirmed and wormed his way out of my arms, jumped to the floor, and danced and pranced around the room with a puppy grin and a tail going faster than the highest setting on a metronome.

His shelter name was Mason. At first, I wanted to name him after the television series called The Chosen, a timeline of Christ's life. A friend suggested the name Chaz. I didn't love it as a first name, but it was perfect as a middle one, and that's how he became Mason Chaz Mahoney.

I wish I could say it was a perfect transition, but it was not. I had to learn to be Mason's mom, to understand his uniqueness, and to teach him to become the dog I needed him to be when it came to some of his quirky behaviors. He's opinionated and would have me throwing a ball to him over and over during every waking hour. He has been known to bark nonstop till he gets his way. He chewed through a kennel and beds and all sorts of things. He wanted to eat anything on our walks, cigarette butts included, but we've somehow made things work.

Three years into our life together, I can say that it's a true toss up as to who was the rescuer and who got rescued. Before Mason came into my life, I was socially isolated without a purpose. I would binge-watch endless shows and movies, eat more than was good for me, or sometimes I wouldn't eat. I spent far too many hours sleeping because at least I didn't have to face endless hours alone. At times I didn't sleep at all.

Mason forced me to have a regular schedule, to get outside in the sun and soak up vitamin D. Getting out and moving with Mason, taking walks in the park or hiking on trails, has helped me manage the chronic pain that often comes with arthritis and age.

Mason has made me laugh and groan and cry. But most of all, Mason has made me feel alive.

Having a dog in my life has shown me that everyone needs a purpose. I think that my God-given purpose is to shower love on those in need, to make them feel loved. Even a little dog.

DOGS OF BROOKSHAVEN
Peggy Frezon

"Old dogs care about you, even when you make mistakes."
— Tom T. Hall

My husband, Mike, and I made a large wooden sign with the name BrooksHaven painted on the front, and hung it prominently in our living room. At the time we made it, there was only a dream. The sign was a promise to ourselves.

Four years earlier, we'd met a dog in a parking lot outside of a pet food store. A rescue worker held the retriever's leash, and he stood with his gaze cast down. He was scrawny, with gangly legs and crooked teeth. His golden fur hung in grimy patches.

"He's perfect," Mike said.

I was not so easily convinced. The poor dog had been abandoned, shuffled between animal shelters in the south, and then transported to a rescue group up north. No one had asked for him. Perhaps I wouldn't have been so hesitant, if it wasn't for his age.

"He's been on his own for a long time. The vet thinks he's eleven," the rescue worker told us, smiling hopefully. It looked like every one of those years had taken a heartbreaking toll on him.

"What do you think?" Mike asked. "Let's get him before someone else does."

I sighed. Puppies went fast. Not so senior dogs. We knelt in front of him and stroked his fur. He didn't budge, as if he'd lost all hope.

"Good boy," I whispered. I wished we could help, but I didn't want to take him, knowing we wouldn't have much time together. We'd fall in love and he'd break our hearts.

Mike put his hand in mine. "He needs us," he said.

That's when I understood. It wasn't about what this dog could do for us. It was about what we could do for him. We could give him a warm, loving home for however long we had together. We could give him the comfort he deserved in his golden years.

We told the rescue worker we'd take him, and the old dog went home with us that very day. As we walked together toward our car, I thought I saw the tip of his tail wag. Maybe he had a little hope after all.

Brooks, as we named him, became a wonderful addition to our family. An older dog, we found, fit perfectly into our lifestyle. He was house trained, never got the urge to chew furniture, and was content with leisurely strolls around the neighborhood. Best of all, he loved just being with us. If I was reading, or gardening, or working on the computer, he was stretched out beside me, his head resting gently on my feet. He had no negative behaviors, no separation anxiety. He knew the secret of being happy with what he had in the moment. We loved him completely.

As you may have guessed, Brooks did break our hearts. He got cancer and died just short of a year later; but it was the best year.

Our story doesn't end there. The day came when our hearts healed, at least a little, and we were ready to rescue another dog. This time, we told ourselves, it would be a younger dog. Maybe a puppy. One who had plenty of years ahead to bond with us and play and to grow up with our grandchildren. We looked at adorable pups at rescue groups' meet-ups. But when it came right down to it, none of them felt right. Something had changed inside of us. Brooks had changed us. We wanted to rescue senior dogs.

The next dog we took in was a nine-year-old golden who'd lived a hard life. We gave him a soft bed, room to run, and the most important thing—unconditional love. Which, of course, he returned a hundredfold.

Our mission grew, one or two dogs at a time. Next, we rescued an old dog, we named him Ernest, who had been neglected and kept in a cage all day and night. When the rescue group worker picked him up, his owner didn't even say goodbye. I promised him he'd never step foot in a cage again.

He proved to be completely trustworthy when left home alone and has never needed to be crated. We took him through training classes and he became a certified therapy dog. He also got cancer, but this time there is a happy ending. He's currently our oldest-lived golden retriever, at fourteen-and-a-half years old!

We continue to rescue homeless senior dogs as long as we can provide them a loving home, healthy food, and proper veterinary care. Our most recent senior is a ten-year-old female. She'd been a breeding mama in deplorable conditions at a puppy mill. When she became too old to produce more puppies, she was considered disposable. Sophie came to us frightened and withdrawn. She's now the sweetest girl who loves attention, and is also on her way to becoming a therapy dog.

We didn't set out to rescue seniors, but there's nothing we'd rather do than give these old dogs a well-deserved retirement home to happily live out their lives. We moved to a new place with a big, green yard for them to explore. And that sign? It hangs in our new living room, just as meaningful and important as the day we made it. Only now it no longer represents a dream. We named our golden retriever retirement home BrooksHaven, after the dog who started it all.

IT STARTED WITH MISTY
Susan E. Mullaney

"No matter how close we are to another person, few human relationships are as free from strife, disagreement, and frustration as is the relationship you have with a good dog.
— Dean Koontz

After I inherited my parent's farm, my husband and I decided to move there. My son suggested that we needed to get a farm dog so, in 2004, that's exactly what we did.

At the time, I was boarding horses, and we had llamas who liked escaping. We reached out to a border collie rescue and went through the adoption approval process. I had several items on my wish list. I wanted a real farm dog, one that had lived on a livestock farm and wouldn't harass horses. I was looking for a dog between four and five years old. They didn't have anything immediately available that fit the description, but I was willing to wait.

Months went by without a match. After six months, I asked what other rescue dogs that they might have ready for me to adopt. The adoption counselor mentioned a dog that was in Maine, which was a doable distance. She'd been living on a horse farm before her family moved out west and left her.

She'd been in rescue for a long time. Since we were approved, they asked if we wanted to drive out and meet him. They didn't need to ask twice. My son made an appointment and drove to Maine. Six hours later, he and Misty arrived back at the farm.

I'd been expecting a smaller dog; she was over sixty pounds, but I could work with that. Misty was black and white, a sort of a brindled color, like a heeler. She was also eight-years-old. That was twice the age I wanted, but she was beautiful, very gentle, and smart.

Misty was a border collie/Aussie/mix with, to my eye at least, some Australian cattle dog thrown in for good measure. I wasn't sure about having a senior dog, but my son said to trust him. He knew she was our dog.

After her family left her in Maine, Misty was fostered by a family who had given up on finding her an adopter. But Misty was just waiting for us. She was exactly what we needed. The rescuer we were working with knew it, too. Misty taught us about herding dogs. She ran the farm, watched over all the animals, patrolled the boundaries twice a day, and alerted me if anything was out of place. And she could herd escaping llamas back into their pen in two minutes or less.

The year after Misty became a part of our family my retired husband was diagnosed with cancer. He went through surgery and a year of chemo. Misty appointed herself his physical therapist. Every afternoon she came for him to do their three-mile walk, rain or shine. Off they went together down to the road around the cranberry bogs. Misty loved to swim in the reservoir herding all the wild geese into the water. My husband's doctor said that the consistent exercise had made a big difference in his recovery.

We only had Misty for four years because of cancer. Six months before she died, we adopted another rescue, Odin, an eighteen-month-old purebred Aussie. He was surrendered because his family lived in a condo and he wouldn't stop growing. Or barking.

Odin was seventy pounds when he came to our farm but he was at least ninety when he turned three. We were exactly what his rescuer was looking for: a farm setting with an older female herder to teach him how to be an Aussie. His first owners had Odin so thoroughly trained, that he refused to run, but Misty knew exactly what Odin needed and she was a superb teacher.

The night before Misty passed away, she insisted on going to the barn to do her job, despite barely being able to breathe. The vet said she'd stay late if I wanted to bring her in to end her suffering. I scheduled it for the next morning so that my son could get there to say goodbye. I spent the night holding her.

My son arrived bright and early at 7:00, and he held her until it was time to leave for the vet. He carried her to the truck for that one last trip. Misty looked out of the window as we drove alongside the cranberry bog where she loved to run. He drove her one last time along the route packed with memories, and she passed away on the seat next to him. We buried her on the hill next to the barn overlooking her llamas and horses.

It started with Misty, but the stories continue. My husband and I retired and moved to a larger hobby farm in Maine and took all of our animals. We added Patches, our third Aussie, and when one of our crew passes, we look for another rescue Aussie. We are so hooked by their intelligence, loyalty, and work ethic that we won't have any other breed now.

We found a wonderful group, Australian Shepherds Furever (ASF), and started working with them online. I was so impressed by ASF and their process, I agreed to foster for them. We also adopted a puppy from them soon after because I really wanted another farm dog to train like Misty. I agreed to take two more puppies at the same time as Digby. And then two more. Then a whole litter. And another litter.

I foster older dogs, the ones who've had some tough breaks and need their confidence rebuilt before finding their forever homes. It can take six months or a year, but it's worth it. When they choose for themselves and find their person, things fall into place like magic.

I have become like that original rescuer who matched us with Misty. I rescue Aussies now, because of Misty, who will forever be my best girl.

OUR PERFECT FOSTER FAIL
Margot Bennett

"Dogs just need you and love, that's all."
— Jennifer Westfeldt

Have you ever wondered how therapy dogs come to be? Therapy dogs must be well-tempered. This means that they are not quick to anger, and do not get stressed out easily. They should enjoy being touched, and not react aggressively if mishandled. That's where I fit into the therapy dog puzzle. For the last twenty-five years I've been a therapy dog puppy raiser and therapy dog team member.

Therapy dogs go with their owners to volunteer in schools, hospitals, nursing homes, and other places. It could be working with a child who is learning to read or visiting a senior in assisted living. Some therapy dogs even work with local law enforcement agencies during times of trauma. Therapy dogs and their owners work together as a team to improve the lives of other people.

I began searching for a puppy when it dawned on me that our current yellow Labrador would not be able to work with me as a therapy dog team member forever. Brisco had three or four years left where we could comfortably visit people. I knew that it would take at least two years to prepare and train a dog for therapy work, so that meant I needed to start the search now.

Then I heard about a litter of Lab puppies that had been left at the county animal shelter. Twelve had been scooped up by a rescue group, and they asked if I would be interested in fostering two of them while I was looking for my next dog.

At the time, all four of my children were living at home, and two of them were old enough to help if I needed extra hands. So Honey and Muffin came home with us. That meant two little white fluffballs to be carried outside to potty, two little white fluff balls to romp and play with each other, and two little white fluffballs to curl up to our older yellow pooch. Thankfully, Brisco welcomed them on his pillow.

Honey found a family, but as is often the case, because puppies are sneaky like that, foster fail happened within three weeks. Muffin, renamed Aspen, began her life with us.

Aspen was different in one key way from the other Labs I had raised or encountered. A true Lab swallows an entire meal whole within ten seconds flat. But not Aspen. While Brisco crunched away, Aspen sniffed her food, circled the dish, backed away, sniffed again, went to the other side of the room, and counted to ten. Then, and only then, did she consider it safe to eat her meal. If a piece of paper fell or a cereal box was opened while she was eating, she'd take off running. She'd eventually come back, sometimes hours later, to finish her food.

When Aspen became old enough, we began taking walks with her and again, I wondered about her background. More like a breeding dog, her relentless pursuit in keeping her family pack together was evident. She'd pant and pull to get to the front kids, who raced ahead of the slower ones, and then circle back and herd us together.

We learned that she had a very strong prey drive and we had to test out all sorts of leashes and harnesses with her. I equate her to a roller coaster going from zero to sixty in less than two seconds when she sees a squirrel, bunny, bike, scooter, or a skateboard. She's the only pup I've ever had that considers skateboard prey. It's probably because it's the most likely of all for her to hear coming towards her. She takes a few steps back to get ready and then lunges forward in an attempt to chase.

Within a few months of watching her reactions and overall demeanor, I realized she was not meant for therapy dog work, and we let her kick back and just be part of the family. I was curious to know if she was not a Lab, what was she? I felt the need to understand her prey drive, her suspicious nature, her desire to pack us together. The DNA test said that she's fifty percent German shepherd, twenty-five-percent Labrador retriever, and twenty-five-percent who knows what. When we added all those numbers together the result was exactly as expected. She's one-hundred-percent ours.

After so many years of raising therapy dogs and having routines, it's fun having a dog that is only expected to love us. We know she has sensitive hearing, especially when she hears a slice of cheese being unwrapped. She comes galloping from the other side of the house for her share.

She always lets Brisco have the first bowl of leftover cereal milk when the kids are done eating breakfast. She likes almond and skim milk equally well.

And then there are the doors. Maybe it's the shepherd in her, but if a doorbell rings she goes into full protect mode, which means loud barking until one of us lets her know all is well. And if the back door creaks open? She races from around the corner and outside, then turns and looks at you to come with her. That's her sign that tennis ball chasing can commence. If said person who opened the back door does not come outside with her? She gives him or her the look of shame, backing up and circling the tennis ball, waiting and whining.

If you grab the tennis ball and say, "Okay, Aspen, I'll throw a few for you," she'll lunge for the ball and run away. If you choose to not go outside with her, she will stare you down through the window, waiting and watching you with a look that says, "How dare you look." If you choose not to cater to her, she will then hunker down by the door and just pout. Point made.

Years passed and the older kids started going away to college. The reunion of them coming home was video worthy. Moaning, butt scratching, fur flying, racing to get her favorite toy to show you. The toy thing came about because she would scratch at our legs when we got home so we taught her to get a toy to bring us. Mounds of soft toys are now left by the door just for her to grab when we get home.

Aspen's quest for adventure has not lightened up as she's aged. During our first vacation in the mountains, she took off after a deer and disappeared long enough for us to be concerned. When she came back her prey drive had been satiated—as had her interest in deer poo. We cleaned up after her for hours after that adventure. She will still take off to go exploring at home now if given the opportunity.

As Brisco neared retirement from therapy work and Aspen settled in more and more, I wanted another way to work with a dog. Since then, I have raised three service dogs, and Aspen has become mom and playmate to the three yellow Labs that have come through our family.

Aspen may not have had the temperament to be the kind of therapy dog who goes to work in an official capacity, but she has forged a path of her own into our hearts. She is devoted to us, has never met a couch she doesn't like, and will continue to mentor other dogs that come through our house to train for service.

STUBBORN IN A GOOD WAY
Rose Maureen

"Even the tiniest poodle or chihuahua is still a wolf at heart."
— Dorothy Hinshaw

When I was just five, my doting father died of a massive heart attack. Mom had always been kindly, yet distracted. After Dad died, my mother spiraled into a depression and began to make poor choices. She claimed it was all because of the stress of being a single parent. Regardless of the reason, she began drinking heavily.

Alcoholism of a parent is a lot for a young child to go through, but then Mom discovered crack, a smokeable form of cocaine. Crack was simple to produce and highly profitable for dealers to develop.

It didn't take long for Mom to become addicted. Soon she used up our savings and began committing crimes in a desperate attempt to buy more drugs. At the height of her addiction, she went to prison for robbery, and I went into the foster care system.

This is a story about dogs, but the choices we make about dogs, and how we raise them, really does reflect our upbringing. Foster care is hard because all any child ever wanted was to be with their natural parents, living a storybook life.

I was an only child who had been raised in a sheltered home, primarily by my devout Catholic father. Being a quiet, bookish girl thrust into an environment with many kids, turned me inward. When I wasn't reading, I watched television or slipped into the movie theater without paying. I loved musicals, but my genre of choice was dog movies.

In *Sounder*, I cried when the poor sharecroppers in the depression-plagued south couldn't find enough to eat. They got help from their hunting dog, which made me want a dog as faithful and loving as him. In *Old Yeller*, the loyalty of the misfit canine forced to defend his family was nothing short of miraculous.

There wasn't a dog movie I didn't love. I knew that one day I would grow up and get a dog as goofy as Snoopy, with the cuteness of Benji and the spunk of Shiloh.

Years passed, with my mother finally succumbing to decades of drug abuse. I eventually married a long-haul truck-driver. We relocated for his job several times, and there was never room or time for my dream dog. I still read dog books, would donate towels to my local shelter, and I loved dog movies. My years of hoping for the dog of my dreams never happened, though I did have a few fish in a tank.

All her life, my daughter Sierra Kendra knew about my desire for a dog. One day she surprised me with a rescue dog for my birthday. I named my apple-headed Chihuahua Harmony Joy.

Chihuahuas are known for their bravado, and my Harmony Joy had more than her share of that spirit. She was fiercely independent and highly territorial. It seemed as if she had taken to heart some small dog handbook that told her to bite strangers and attack other dogs, no matter their size.

I enrolled her in a group training class, and we were asked to leave as she would not stop nipping at everyone's ankles. We tried a smaller group so she could learn to socialize with other dogs and their humans. After two sessions we were given a refund

I put a muzzle on my little problem child for the third class, and she hated it. Stubborn to the core, she sat, refusing to even walk when instructed. She was a total washout at dog training, but I refused to give up on Harmony Joy.

A few weeks later I paid a neighbor who volunteered at an animal rescue to help me to train her. Harmony Joy bit her wrist, so I decided to take a break from classes. I felt like a dog mom failure. She would never be Lassie, saving me from falling into a well, or rambunctious and fun like Beethoven when he engaged with others.

We went to a veterinarian who explained that although our dog was physically in good shape, she had fear-based anxiety. Medication could help, but she might never change into a cuddly lap dog.

I took this on as a problem I could fix. I read books, watched YouTube videos, and followed advice from the Dog Whisperer and others. If one thing didn't work, I'd try another. Rewards, clickers, structured play time, and consistent commands all failed to some degree or another.

I started going to local dog shows to see what a good dog acted like, but despite my efforts, Harmony Joy refused to be social. The more I pushed Harmony Joy to change into the dog of my dreams, the more shut down she became. She only came out of her hiding places to eat, drink, or to potty. As soon as she was done, off she would scamper back to my closet or under the bed. If I shut the closet door before she made it inside or dragged her from under the bed, she would turn her back on me, hang her head, and refuse to make eye contact.

Some of my friends suggested I find a shelter that would take her. Because she was snarly, I was afraid a different owner might mistreat her. I made up my mind that no one deserves to be given up on no matter how hard they are to love.

My compromise was to keep Harmony fed and safe but to stop trying to make her socially acceptable.

When Harmony Joy had been with me for about five years, I got diagnosed with an auto immune disease called sarcoidosis. Sarcoidosis is a chronic condition which could result in the deterioration of an affected organ. I had complications with my spleen, eyes, lungs, and heart. Overnight I was bed-ridden and using oxygen.

The goal of the medications was remission, but the side effects created new symptoms, and I felt even worse. One day while I was in my bed wondering what was the point of fighting to breathe, I noticed Harmony Joy sitting quietly and watching me. She had come out of my closet without my begging.

I did not grab her or bombard her with a bunch of toys as I had done before. Day by day she came out from under my bed and got closer, and by the end of the week, she had become the lapdog of my dreams. During the height of my illness she rarely left my side.

Getting to know her, I began to understand that the naughty label was unfair. Before I became ill, I was very often too high-energy for Harmony Joy. Trying to force her to be something she was never meant to be was clearly intimidating and overwhelming to my furry friend. When I was in foster care I acted out from a place of self-protection. My actions seemed to others as if I were a fighter, but I only wanted to be loved, even when I was unlovable.

Once I let go of my unrealistic explanations, she became my side-kick and best friend. When the disease forced me into to the hospital, I worked hard and did whatever was needed so I could get home, because she needed me.

She greeted me with a lick and a wag of her tail when I got home. She never felt the need to be liked by everyone else, but she loved me.

We were together a wonderful thirteen years before she died peacefully in her sleep. Our life together wasn't the fairy tale I had expected when I got a dog. Instead, it was reality. We rescued each other in a beautiful story of love, commitment, and tenacity.

UNEXPECTED HEROES
Diane Huff Pitts

*Peer into your loving dog's eyes and you
will have seen true trust and loyalty.*
— Jeff Tikari

I saw him between the bread and ice cream aisle. The lanky man appeared scruffy around the edges and crowned with a dingy Vietnam vet cap. At his sandaled feet stood a white ghost of a dog, content to wait until her master chose the right bread from the top shelf. Her soothing chocolate eyes met mine without fear or concern.

"What a beautiful dog," I said. "May I ask her breed?"

"Great white Pyrenees," he announced. A flicker of pride widened his hazel eyes. "Her name's Lady."

Drawn by a family trait to love all canines, my fingers itched to touch her. "May I pet her?" I paused. "Service dog?"

Lady's ears perked up. As if she understood my request, she padded over within stroking-distance and sniffed my khakis.

I looked at her owner for permission. "Smells my two pups."

"Sure, you can pet her. She's as gentle as they come." The gentleman gave her latitude with the leash. "Lady's more of a rescue dog than a service dog, but I take her with me because she has acute separation anxiety."

What a twist—a veteran taking care of an anxious dog. That was hard to fathom since Lady melted into the floor to the point of laziness. I rubbed her shaggy head, marveling at the depths of her dark eyes.

My curiosity wouldn't let me leave; I wanted to keep this man talking without being intrusive.

"I'm Diane. Mind if I ask your name?"

"No problem. I'm Jerry."

"How old is Lady?"

By this time, without one hint of anxiety, the beautiful dog stretched prone in the aisle and planted her head between my feet.

"She's three." He laughed. "She's through sniffing, and now she's laying claim to you. You're 'found.'"

I sensed Jerry wanted to talk about Lady and their adventures. "How did you find each other?"

Settling in, he pushed his buggy toward the ice cream side of the aisle so shoppers could pass.

"I've never had a dog. But I ran into someone with a litter of great Pyrenees puppies. Lady was the runt of the litter."

He looked down affectionately before continuing. "I've seen her brother, and he's about 150 pounds heavier than this girl. Pyrenees are herders and rescuers." Jerry repositioned his cap. "I'm all about helping, and figured I wasn't too old to train with a dog. We were at Quantico and a few other prep sites."

Glancing down at Lady, I wondered if this languid dog would be excited about anything. "What kind of rescues have you done?"

"Lady's specialty is locating kids, but she hunts for anyone." He straightened his shoulders. "In the last few years, FEMA called us for 175 disaster sites."

Taking in the magnitude of Jerry's explanation, I thought of recent global devastations.

"I could see the two of you headed to Turkey and Syria after the earthquakes."

Jerry nodded. "That's a fact, but FEMA hasn't called us in a few months. Last call was Ukraine. Just didn't work out."

The moment enveloped me. Shoppers pushed by, but I recognized none of it. I savored being in the presence of these unlikely heroes.

"I could talk all day." The corner of his mouth lifted and matched the quick gleam in his eye. "I better let you shop."

SUNFLOWER LOYALTY • 109

"You made my day, Jerry. Thanks for telling me your story." Sensing I included her, Lady lifted her majestic head. Her gaze exhibited a wisdom far beyond her years.

As they sauntered away, I pondered the irony of Jerry the war veteran—a hero in his own right—and Lady, a hero in two ways. Not only had she rescued the unfortunate, but Lady also rescued a man. Jerry wanted to be needed. To matter. To improve the world. Lady made it happen.

These two heroes left me speechless between the bread and ice cream aisle; their quiet greatness changed me.

MADE TO SERVE
Xochitl Dixon

"You'll never get the dog that you want;
you'll always get the dog that you need."
—Cesar Milan

In July 2018, my husband, Alan, left me in California and moved to Wisconsin. I planned on joining him in August. We were following God to the Midwest for a job opportunity, or so we thought. He stayed in a hotel, while I searched online for a home and a new team of specialists to help with my medical needs. In 1992, I had injured my spine, so I live in constant pain. I needed a support system before I moved. So, I prayed and posted prayer requests on social media.

A person I knew introduced me to Carmen Leal. During our first conversation, we realized she and her husband lived only twenty minutes from our new home.

"I have to finish writing these doggy bios tonight," she said. "Tell Alan we'll pick him up for dinner on Saturday."

Before we hung up, she sent me photos of three puppies. One looked so much like our senior dog Jazzy that I had to text the photo to my husband.

He immediately texted back. *NO PUPPIES!*

Carmen laughed when I told her about Alan's response. "These pups aren't ready for adoption yet," she said. "He has time to change his mind."

"That will never happen," I said. I didn't try to convince Alan to adopt the puppy. But I didn't delete her picture from my phone either.

Almost two weeks later, I flew across the country. The following day, Carmen and Gary picked us up for lunch with a stop to see the puppies.

I teared up as soon as we pulled into the NEW PAWSibilities parking lot. I stood in the lobby weeping and laughing, as the wiggly pup licked my face and tinkled down the front of my shirt.

"This is why we do what we do," said Carmen.

I named our puppy Callie, short for California. Why? After spending one night in Wisconsin, I wanted to return home as soon as possible!

God used Callie to help make life more bearable, less lonely and depressing. But my first few days in the Midwest tested my faith and my marriage.

Our new home was not all the realtors had promised. My husband was either too busy or too irritable. I couldn't find a doctor who understood my complex back injury. My rambunctious border collie/treeing walker coonhound mix resisted my best training techniques. My grumpy senior dog hated our new addition to the family. As the cold increased, my pain increased. Within the first month of my time in Wisconsin, the creek next to our home flooded, mosquitoes swarmed every time we stepped outside, and a dozen tornadoes devastated portions of our community. Then, someone told me that winter in Wisconsin lasted well into the Spring!

How could I finish a manuscript I was writing about trusting God in the waiting seasons in life, when I could barely trust Him in the day-to-day grind?

I thanked God for blessing us with good things amid the hard stuff, too. Though my son, Xavier, wasn't happy about our leaving California, at least he was doing well on his own. I eventually found a good doctor, a good vet, and made some good friends.

Though I couldn't get Callie into a training class until February, I taught her how to walk on leash before the middle of September. At first, I could only walk to the end of the block and back. Soon, we started walking to the park, a few blocks away. Then, we walked to the neighborhood school, almost a mile from our home and across the street from a woman who we came to know as Grandma Jan.

Walking with Callie on my right side, instead of walking with my cane on my left side, helped me keep my balance but didn't cause me to have as many muscle spasms. Though I was still in pain, while walking and after walking with Callie, I was able to walk more, walk further, and recover quicker. I shared this with my new friend, Callie's trainer at the vet, Jill.

"That's amazing," said Jill, writing a phone number on a slip of paper. "Jake Guell is a professional service dog trainer and the owner of Tails for Life. They're fifteen minutes from your house."

Shortly after meeting with us, Jake evaluated Callie. He warned us that a high percentage of mixed breeds failed the service dog training program. We couldn't be sure about Callie's temperament under working conditions or her desire to work. We had no idea what she had been through prior to adoption or how her experiences would impact her training. Still, Jake assured us that Callie was smart and seemed eager to please.

In our ministry together Callie and I would be telling people about Jesus which Jake thought was an added bonus. Callie was accepted into the next service dog training class. However, those pups had been training with Jake since birth. So, Callie would be a full year behind when she started the program.

The odds were stacked high against my sweet Callie Mae. Still, I didn't doubt for one second that God had made her to serve me in this way.

Shortly before we began the program, my doctor found a medication that he believed could provide pain relief in my upper thoracic area. Up until then, nothing had worked. "Insurance won't cover the treatment," he said. "You'll have to pay out of pocket. If it works, you'll have to repeat the treatment every three months."

"The pain in my upper back feels like an ice pick jabbing into my spine. I have excruciating muscle spasms and debilitating headaches every day. I live hunched over, afraid of people touching me. Hugs hurt. Standing, sitting, lying on my left side hurts. Breathing hurts," I said. "I don't know how we'll be able to afford the procedure. But if this works . . . it'll be worth the sacrifice."

After praying with my husband, I asked Jake to take Callie off the list since I no longer felt we could afford to have her trained.

Jake encouraged me to share my story on Facebook. "Let's see if people will donate to help you pay for Callie's training," he said. "I don't do usually do this, but I'll work out a payment plan for the balance. I think a service dog will help you."

I cried. A lot. I thanked Jake, praised God, and prayed before sharing our story on my blog and on social media. Donors from around the world, mostly strangers, paid Callie's service dog training fees in full— within three days!

I kept readers updated online as Callie completed her training. I shared our challenges, our stumbles, and our victories. I shared prayer requests and praises. I encouraged others as I wrote our story in articles and devotional compilations.

In August 2019, Callie joined me at the Our Daily Bread Ministries offices in Grand Rapids, Michigan to celebrate the release of my first book, *Waiting for God: Trusting Daily in God's Plan and Pace*, the book I wrote when we moved to Wisconsin. She lay at my feet as I shared a message of hope from the podium. Everyone was witnessing Callie's first event as my service dog. One woman said, "Callie is a natural." But I knew that Callie was a miracle, made to serve and sent to me by God.

Before we left the office, my editor surprised me with a sneak peek of the illustrations for my first children's picture book, *Different Like Me,* scheduled for release later that year. The team decided to feature Callie as the service dog with one of the main characters in the book. Since its release, God has been using *Different Like Me*, now translated into Spanish, Simplified Chinese, and Dutch, to help readers around the world celebrate our differences and our sameness as His beautifully and intentionally unique image-bearers.

God continues to give me opportunities to advocate for inclusion, equity, and justice as I share my book, which portrays diverse children with and without disabilities working and playing side by side. He allows me to share how I wrote the original manuscript for *Different Like Me* in 2001, almost twenty years before it was published. I was a new Christian trying to help my son respond in love after another student called him a racial slur at school. I share how I started submitting the manuscript in 2010 and signed the contract with Our Daily Bread Publishing in 2018.

God didn't allow *Different Like Me* to be released until August 2020—only three months after the murder of George Floyd. In God's perfect timing, when our country—when I—needed the gentle and biblical reminder to choose love over hate, God sent Callie the service dog to help me choose love over hate. He gave us *Different Like Me* to share with readers around the world online and in person, so we could help them do the same.

As quickly and unexpectedly as God led us to Wisconsin in 2018, He brought us back to California in September 2020. I began working on two more children's books that would feature Callie the Service Dog. In *What Color is God's Love?* Callie and her handler help readers process their emotions in the safety of His loving presence, as they learn more about His unchanging character while they practice loving one another.

In *Wonderfully, Marvelously Brown*, Callie and her biracial handler inspire readers to use their imagination to explore five regions in the United States, celebrating the richness of America's diverse communities in search of the perfect shade of brown God chose for their skin —exploring every hue from the lightest ivory to the darkest ebony. We're working on more picture books and devotionals that encourage and empower readers to love God and all their beautifully diverse neighbors.

As I continue struggling with my pain and fatigue management, Callie serves faithfully by my side. God blessed her with a quirky personality, one border collie flippy ear, and one treeing walker coonhound floppy ear. She is loving and silly, but also ready to work hard once I snap on her service dog vest. She helps me balance and brace myself. She applies pressure therapy when needed. She picks up items I drop. She carries, retrieves, and delivers items. We continue working together, sometimes falling short, and are always ready to learn.

Callie is a mutt, dumped in a kill-shelter, discarded as if she had no value or purpose. By God's grace, Carmen Leal and the NEW PAWSabilities team rescued her and brought us together. Jake and Amanda Guell and the Tails for Life trainers invested in her and in me as if we were family. Strangers donated toward her training. God's beautifully diverse people from around the world prayed and are still praying for us as we work together. Every person who supports us is a partner in ministry, adding value simply because they exist and remind us that we have value simply because we exist.

Though Callie sometimes still struggles with focusing, especially when her hound-dog nose tempts her toward distraction, she is the perfect service dog for me. As I look back on our journey, I can see how God brought us together. Callie is made to serve. She is perfectly different and special, valued and loved, exactly how God created her—just like I am, and just like you are!

CHAPTER FIVE

HYDRANGEA
GRATITUDE

GIRL ON THE RUN

"Gardens are a form of autobiography."
— Sydney Eddison

Earlier this year we were invited to be one of six homes on our town's Garden Walk, and we were trying to keep everything alive during a long and unwelcome dry spell. We'd wake up early, and Gary would use the soaker hose on all of the ornamental bushes, and I'd go out front and weed.

I need to remind you that I am not a real gardener nor do I play one on television. Last year we hired a native landscaping company to rip out the terrace sod, which was a hot mess of weeds, and replace it with native plants and grasses. There were places that had not grown in yet and the weeds were taking over with a vengeance. I had to protect our investment, so pulling those invaders every day in the morning became my habit.

On this particular day when it was already hotter than I would have liked, I got dressed for my daily search and destroy mission. I decided to wear this super cute dress with a crisscross top. When I was getting dressed, I debated about putting on the one garment we women all hate: underwire bras. There was a lot of bending to get all that spurge, the bane of my summertime, and since it was my yard, I didn't really care what anyone had to say about my attire. Besides, bra or no bra, the dress was cute, cool, and comfortable.

I went to the front yard and began working on the terrace next to the street. Weeding, weeding, weeding. I was in my zone, and I heard a honk.

"Oh, how nice," I thought. "Someone is honking to say thank you for making our community beautiful."

My weed bag filled up nicely, despite the ground being as hard as cement from the lack of rain. I heard another honk. "Wow! People love my yard," I said to myself, as I moved to the next area.

By the third honk, I was convinced I would win a terrace of the year award if there was such a thing. Then I looked down.

And that's when I learned that people didn't care about the yard. In fact, I bet they had not noticed my efforts at all. There I was, in my cute sundress during the morning rush hour, such as we have in our small city, and one of the girls had escaped!

At that point I turned my back to the street and kept on weeding. Some things are more important than dignity. I still weed every day in front of my house, but I don't wear that dress.

As I type this story, I'm reminded of another almost catastrophe that happened at the convention center a few years ago. Yes, it involves dogs.

The organizer of the annual Senior Expo in our town asked me if we might be able to bring puppies from the rescue and set up a kennel in the lobby. That year we had four or five adorable puppies, along with volunteers to help people into the kennel to sit and play with them. Some less than agile seniors opted to have the pups handed to them to hug and enjoy.

The following year, we didn't have any puppies, but we did have a couple small dogs available for adoption. Since we had a number of volunteers scheduled to come, we also brought some medium dogs to be walked throughout the lobby for people to meet.

Gary unloaded the van and my volunteers had not arrived. Rollie, a ten-pound Chihuahua/terrier went into the kennel. While waiting for the volunteers to arrive, I gripped the leashes tethering the two hound/mix pups and the one cattle dog/mix. That's when I learned that when you bring dogs that are too large to go inside the kennel, it's probably best to not wear a floor-length skirt. I guess the dogs thought it was a toy of some sort.

People began coming into the Expo as the three dogs each took a bit of my skirt in their teeth and began pulling. Jolly the cattle dog was having a blast with that skirt as she pulled, and the leashes became intertwined and wrapped around my legs.

Jolly tugged, and I felt the elasticized waistband begin to slip, causing me to remember the image of a puppy tugging at the bathing suit bottom of a little girl in a vintage suntan lotion commercial.

As my skirt slipped further down my backside, two women walking by rescued me, each taking a leash—well, they had to unwind the leashes and dogs to get them separated, but I was able to stay upright, I did not flash the crowd, and my volunteers arrived.

We all had a good laugh, and with my dignity intact, I greeted the volunteers. I have never been more grateful that the two ladies rescued this damsel in distress.

A few weeks later, it was time to plan what we'd be doing in the garden that year. The snow had melted, and we decided to tackle the vanilla strawberry hydrangea in front of our house. This majestic bush starts off white in the spring and then turns red, exactly as the name implies. It's the best of the few plants still there before we bought the house. The owner had never pruned it and so it failed to teach its full potential.

When members of the online group of Wisconsin gardeners suggested that it was important to prune them, I was convinced we'd kill it. I went onto YouTube and saw a few do-it-yourself tutorials, and Gary did a great job. What a difference a little fertilizer and pruning can make.

Too many dogs never get the training they need and deserve. I made so many mistakes as Coconut's mom, but I decided that spending time and money with a professional trainer was a must. I am so grateful to our trainer for helping us to bring out the best in our dog.

I think if dogs could talk to us, the number one thing that they would share is that they are grateful to have a person, a home, and love. They are also grateful for the training they receive, because life is better for everyone, them included. The cool thing is that they might not be able to talk to us in words we understand, but they show us their gratitude every day.

My dog gives me countless doggy kisses every day. His smiles bring me such joy and shows me unconditional love preferring to stay close to me no matter what I'm doing. His tail wagging is just one more way he expresses his happiness and thankfulness.

I was pretty grateful that I didn't cause a bigger scene while pulling weeds and corralling dogs. I'm even more grateful that dogs are such a major part of our lives.

A STAR NAMED LUCY
Chris Trollinger

"He is your friend, your partner, your defender, your dog.
You are his life, his love, his leader. He will be yours,
faithful and true, to the last beat of his heart.
You owe it to him to be worthy of such devotion."
— Agnes Repplier

About three months after the death of our old cocker spaniel, Maddie, Gene and I decided it was time to adopt another four-legged family member. We'd always opted for six-week-old pups, but this time we talked about getting an older dog, one who just needed a good home. Even though we had successfully trained the young ones and had loved them all, the thought of potty training and chewed shoes and every-thing else that goes with puppies was more than we wanted to take on at our age.

In 1997 there were still pet listings in newspapers, and one Sunday I found an ad for the perfect dog. I knew I needed to get over there quickly because a small, Yorkshire terrier, who was only two years old, gentle, and housebroken would not last long.

On Tuesday morning, I called the owner who assured me the dog was still there along with her other pup, a Chesapeake Bay retriever/ Labrador mix with unspecified special needs. I jumped into the car that Tuesday afternoon convinced I'd come home with a lap dog that day.

I was eager to meet the little terrier only to learn that another family had arrived before me and was taking her home. I started walking back to the car when the woman asked me if I would be interested in meet-ing the remaining dog, one that was not even remotely on my radar.

She was so persistent that I said yes, fully intending to leave right away. And then I heard her story.

"We raised her until she was a year old," explained the desperate woman. "We gave her to my daughter and her husband, who lived on a farm fifty miles away. We thought living on a farm was perfect for such a large dog."

Star was now three and had anything but an idyllic life on the farm. The desperate woman told me that she had not known that her son-in-law was abusive to both his wife and their dog. A couple of months earlier, he had tried to harm the woman while in a drunken rage. Her daughter escaped with the baby, leaving the dog to fend for herself.

The family didn't find out what happened to the dog until later, but as her owner was trying to escape, Star jumped to protect her and was stabbed with a knife. After the man fled the scene, Star began the fifty-mile journey back to her first home. The injured dog had been on the road for several weeks. She almost made it when, within blocks of her former house, she collapsed near a gas station on the interstate.

As she described the scene and shared the gas station's name and location, my heart skipped a beat. I knew the very dog she was describing.

Two weeks after losing Maddie, Gene had come home from work distraught. He had passed that gas station and had seen a dog staggering in and out of traffic. Even from a distance he could tell that the Lab mix of some sort was starving and had been beaten. He, along with several other people, had stopped and were trying to divert the rush hour traffic to save the dog.

Finally, the exhausted and terrified pup collapsed in front of the gas station. People tried to come near, but even in her weakened state, she would not let anyone approach After a bit, a woman came by and said she recognized the animal as her neighbor's missing dog. The frightened animal offered no resistance when the woman called out the name, Star. She became docile and allowed the woman to load her into her truck.

When the story ended, I knew Star had a new home. My husband had been worried about the fate of that dog every day since witnessing the incident. Not only had she survived an unbelievable trek trying to get to safety, but Gene was there for the last bit of her journey.

The look on Gene's face when I came home with the seventy-six-pound black and white dog was one of utter amazement.

"Good Lord," he exclaimed. "She looks just like the Lab I saw at the gas station, the one nearly got killed in traffic that day."

I quickly gave him the details of how I left earlier that day to pick up a lapdog but came home with anything but. Once the remarkable pieces of the puzzle fell into place there was no question that God had brought Star into our lives.

Once I knew Gene was ready to give Star a home, I told him that there was one more part of the story he needed to hear. There was another reason why the woman had been so insistent about my meeting Star and hearing her story. Somewhere along the way, our new dog had gotten heartworm disease and the couple had no money for her care. They were hoping that whoever adopted her would be able to pay for her treatment so that they would not have to put her to sleep.

As with any rescue, there were some bumps in the road the biggest being that whenever Gene got near her, she cowered in fear. It took a while, but Gene realized that wearing his baseball cap terrified her. We reasoned that the man who abused her probably wore a baseball cap to shield his head from the sun while farming. Gene packed away all of his hats and, over the next few weeks, Star warmed up to him.

After several rounds of heartworm treatment, Star's health improved, and our girl quickly learned that Gene was her champion. He held her and cuddled her through all the misery she had to endure with the treatments.

After a couple of weeks, Gene decided a name change was in order because she wasn't responding when he called her. He decided the man must have used the name when beating her. She seemed to associate the name Star with pain. Sure enough she instantly came to accept the name Lucy, and it stuck. We never mentioned her old name again.

Even though I was the one who had rescued her, Gene was obviously Lucy's best friend. She snuggled by his chair when he came home and was unwilling to sleep anywhere except beside him in the bed. He didn't have the heart to make her sleep on the floor. She quickly wormed her way into every fabric of our lives.

As the years went by, Lucy became as dear to us as any dog we have ever owned. While she would never completely regain her health, she was the perfect companion for us. She had the sweetest face, which oozed love and affection.

In the summer of 2003, her kidneys began to fail. They had been damaged in her earlier years of abuse, and it would finally prove irreversible. But even though she was becoming frailer, she still managed one last heroic deed before her star burned out.

In early October she had gotten into a habit of jumping up and licking Gene's neck while shivering and whining. Neither of us understood this new behavior, but after talking about it, Gene admitted that he had a sore in his mouth and that his neck hurt.

I finally managed to convince him to see a dentist who recommended an immediate biopsy. My husband tested positive for oral cancer, which required extensive surgery. Gene lived another two years we might not have had if Lucy had not alerted us.

Lucy's earthly light burned out on July 30, 2004 and, while that was a difficult time, I will always know that the last year and a half of sharing my life with Gene was thanks to Lucy's persistence.

I like to think there is a star in the heavens above us burning brightly each night — a star named Lucy.

BRANDY, THE LICKING MACHINE
Sally Apokedak

"Sometimes you don't need words to feel better;
you just need the nearness of your dog."
— Natalie Lloyd

I have always had dogs. We've bought them from breeders, and we've adopted them from shelters. We've kept strays that followed us home and have taken in dogs from friends who had to give them up. Always, always we've had dogs. Big dogs, little dogs, hairy dogs, bald dogs—we've had them all, over the years.

So it came as a big surprise to me to realize, when I became an empty nester, that I had never really had a dog of my own. As a child I'd shared my dogs with all my brothers and sisters. And as an adult the dogs had always "belonged" to the kids. Oh, sure. I fed them and loved them, of course. But they were always chosen by others, or chosen as gifts for someone in the family. None of them were really mine.

So one day shortly after my daughter moved out, taking her dog with her, I decided I'd get a dog for myself.

My son took me to the local shelter. I didn't have a specific breed in mind. But I wanted a young dog—one I could socialize and train.

The shelter had no young puppies. One dog was a possible fit—a Dutch shepherd my son liked. She was seven months old, and she jumped into his arms, licking him all over. And that was enough for me to decide I was taking a hard pass on her—too old and such a licker! She was definitely not the dog I was looking for.

So we decided to leave without adopting a dog—after all, adoption is a big commitment. You have to take care of the animal for years, whether you want to or not. And, while I don't expect any dog to be perfect, I wanted to get a dog I would love. And at the very least, one I was compatible with.

And incessant licking was not something I wanted to live with for the next twelve years.

My son took me back to the shelter the following week. Same situation. No young puppies. But there was the poor, lonely dog who just wanted to lick my son to death when he held her. She simply could not keep her tongue in her mouth.

But she was so lonely and so sweet and obviously very loving. I took her card, ready to go adopt her. There was no other likely candidate there. Maybe this dog was my dog?

And then I thought about that licking again, and I put the card back.

I looked at all the other dogs again. No other dogs there would work for me. And this time, it was supposed to be all about me when it came to choosing my dog. Key words: My. Dog.

I took the licking machine's card again, and I headed for the front desk.

But that tongue! I was pretty sure it would drive me crazy.

I took the card back and put it back on her cage.

My son got frustrated and told me he'd be waiting in the truck for me.

I started to follow my son out. Because, after all, I just did *not* need a seven-month-old dog that licked people to death.

But before I got to the door a thought popped into my head. "You might not need her, but she might need you."

And so I went back, got her card, and took it to the front desk.

And—I have thanked God so many times that I made that decision.

The dog I thought I didn't need, turned out to be the perfect dog for me. So smart. Housebroken fast. Rides in the car with me with no issues— no drooling or whining and getting car sick. She walks with me several miles a day. She's completely devoted to me and will protect me from all danger, especially from evil bicyclists and joggers. (Thankfully, she will sit and let them pass without attacking them if I tell her they are okay.)

And the excessive licking? Well the first thing I taught her was "no licking." And she complies with that command, though it pains her. Seven years later, I still have to tell her sometimes. She sleeps with me through the night, and she's in my lap (all fifty pounds of her) during the day as well because I work from home, and I bought a big enough chair to share with her. And because of this close proximity, she is constantly tempted to steal a lick here and a lick there. But I see her coming and tell her no, and she gets a little guilty look on her face and pulls her tongue back into her mouth.

She was here, lying on my lap, as I wrote this. And she didn't lick once. She didn't even try. So I began to second guess myself. I thought, *She really doesn't have a licking addiction. Maybe I'm not being totally honest writing about my sweet girl's licking problem. She's really like Mary Poppins: practically perfect in every way. She's really pretty much over the licking stuff.*

And as I was thinking maybe I needed to revise this story and tone down my accusation about excessive licking, Sweet Brandy hopped off my lap and trotted out the living room to see my sister who is visiting for Thanksgiving. And immediately I heard my sister saying, "No licking."

GOD SPELLED BACKWARD
Quentin Wood

Life is about bringing love to others. It's about giving
people the ability to turn their lives around."
— Sister Pauline Quinn

I was born in Canada and spent much of my formative years there. In a perfect world, no matter your country or state of origin, adults look back on their childhood as a time filled with wonderful memories. And while I do have some good memories, my childhood was far from perfect.

The details of the abuse I suffered had nothing to do with my parents and others in my family. In fact, they were unaware of what was happening because I remained silent. They never had a chance to help me, which I am sure they would have a had I spoken up.

As a result of the way I was treated, I believed I was an outcast and had little or no worth. After I graduated from high school, my life became a cautionary tale for other teens as I experimented with drugs, alcohol, and an increasingly risky life style. Never believing I belonged anywhere where I could be accepted, I was always looking for that next party and that next high. I figured as long as I faked it, I would find some semblance of acceptance.

I moved in 2000 to be closer to the Wisconsin part of my family. Unless you identify why you are the way you are and work through those problems, you can never really reinvent from yourself no matter how far you run. I was still Quentin, that abused little boy no one had room for in their circle.

In 2006 those valueless feelings caught up with me, and I committed a terrible crime. Every day I'd wake up wondering if this was the day someone would come knocking at my door with a pair of handcuffs. After close to 3,650 days, it happened. In 2015 I was convicted, and I began serving six years of incarceration followed by three years of community supervision.

People ask me about my crime, and I simply tell them that my crime was not being willing to become the man I knew I could be. I had hurt someone, and I was crushed. I let my kids down, my family, and others who had tried to help me over the years. The face I saw in the mirror confirmed all of the self-defeating beliefs I had carried for so long.

In prison, I no longer had the option of drugs, alcohol, and partying to chase those feelings away. By the time I landed at the Oshkosh Correctional Facility, I was contemplating suicide. Wouldn't the world be better off without me in it?

But I didn't want to die, if for no other reason than my death would only cause more suffering. I had hurt the victim, their family, and everyone in my life. How could I ever begin to turn myself around, to forgive myself for all the pain my recklessness had caused?

Another inmate, whom I will call Brother Li, offered to help me. For the rest of my days, I will never forget the words he said that began my road to healing. One day I was walking with him around the yard, me moping and feeling sorry for myself, Brother Li smiling in the sun.

"How can you smile? There's nothing to be cheerful about," I said to this man who had already served more time than my complete sentence. "There is no reason to be happy here, and yet you seem content.

"Quentin," he said. "Listen closely because I will only share this once. Look around you. Ninety percent of the men here spend their days with a chip on their shoulder, seeing their time here as only punishment. These men have no hope."

I stood in the yard on a beautiful sunny day wondering where this conversation was going. I saw myself in Brother Li's description of the vast number of men I encountered each day.

With a twinkle in his eye, and that megawatt smile, he looked at me and waited. He wanted me to be ready to not only listen, but to hear the words he was about to share.

"Being accountable for the choices you made in your past is a big part of becoming the man you are meant to be," Brother Li said. "Real change begins with honesty. It is up to you to either spend your time feeling horrible and blaming everyone else for the choices you made that landed you here, or you can change."

At that moment something in me shifted, as he continued.

"You have the choice to see this place another way. This place can be a temple of healing and learning. And you can choose to utilize everything available to you here, to make the changes you want to make and heal yourself from the wounds of your past."

Those few minutes walking with Brother Li changed my life. After that day, I threw myself into every opportunity I could. I signed up for every program offered, whether it was required or not. I asked how could I truly be of service to the world around me and not just do things that looked good to cast myself in a better light as I had in the past. That is when dogs first entered my life.

The Oshkosh Correctional Institution has a dog training program, and I had seen the selected men working with dogs around the prison. To be honest, up to that point in my life, I had never really given dogs much thought. I had never owned one nor had I been close to any of my friends' pets. I had yet to experience the bond a person can have with an animal and how a dog can change a person's life. All that changed the day I was chosen to join the program.

This program had some of the strictest criteria for admission. I learned that many men had to apply numerous times before being accepted, and most of those who applied were turned down. I don't know what the entrance panel saw in me that made them offer me a place the first time I applied, but I am so thankful they did.

My entire life had been about everyone wanting something from me. It was different with dogs. They never asked for or expected anything in return. The unconditional love and nonjudgmental attention these wonderful animals gave to people, regardless of what they had done in their lives, had the power to change everything.

The puppies came to us when they were between twelve and fourteen weeks old. One of the interesting things is the dogs lived with us in our cells, and we cared for the them twenty-four hours a day. The men in the program, myself included, were coached by Journey Together Service Dog, Inc. With their help we raised and taught these dogs all the behaviors they would need to be service dogs.

During the eighteen months to two years they stayed with us, the goal was to raise and train service dogs that would improve the quality of life for people who had very unique challenges. I was absolutely fascinated, and knowing I was making a difference in the dog's future person's life gave me hope.

When a dog graduated from the program, part of our job included teaching their new forever partners how to maintain the high-level, custom-tailored behaviors the dog had learned.

As the days turned into weeks and then into months and eventually into years, I began to feel a sense of purpose and self-worth for the first time in my life. Over time, as I learned more about canine behavior and how to communicate with and to train dogs, my passion for working with them grew.

I had never been a person who had helped anyone in a tangible, life-changing way. People began sharing their stories with us and, for the first time ever, I realized I had been put on this earth to serve. We received letters from recipients sharing about their companion comforting them during a panic attack. Then there were veterans with prosthetic limbs that were able to live full lives because of their service dogs, and the visually impaired learning to navigate the physical world, thanks to their dog.

One day a Dominican nun by the name of Sister Pauline Quinn came to visit our program. As a young woman, Sister Pauline had experienced much trauma and homelessness. Once she discovered that the unconditional love of a dog helped her to feel safe and self-confident, she launched one of the first prison puppy programs in the United States, which inspired similar programs across the country.

Sister Pauline spoke to us of forgiveness and change. I distinctly remember her words when she said that we could find forgiveness and peace through the work we did training dogs to achieve their purpose. She reminded us that though we must take accountability for our past, it did not have to define us any longer. We had the power to change the lives of others through working with these dogs.

Sister Pauline told us that through God's forgiveness we could begin to forgive ourselves. It was up to us if we wanted to begin our own journey of healing as we learned how to be of service to others.

Sister Pauline had brought her service dog with her. He was a beast of a Rottweiler, yet he was as gentle as a spring breeze. We were asked to put on a total blackout blindfold and trust him to lead us around the block, up and down stairs, and through crowds and doors. It was both a frightening and exciting experience. The exercise really allowed us to see what some of our clients experienced every day and to know how we trained dogs improved their quality of life.

I am reintegrating into society, and my nearly five years in the program still continues to bless me every day. The purpose-driven and fulfilling work I found in prison continues outside the prison walls. With the help of Defy Ventures and the University of Wisconsin, I have opened a pet dog services business, helping everyday pet owners improve their relationship with their pups.

Coming back into the community with the stigma of being justice-impacted carries many challenges. By continuing my work with dogs and seeing the lives of my clients improve, my life has become changed in ways I never would have imagined.

I wake up excited to face each day. I hope to grow my business and to employ other justice-impacted individuals who have been through dog training programs and found the same passion and fulfillment as I have.

Training puppies and young dogs and helping them to find their purpose is how I found mine. The lessons I teach dogs are what parents know their children need in our not-so-perfect world. We all must learn to love, to trust, to obey, and to live with joy every single day of our lives.

Thanks to being chosen to participate in the Oshkosh Correctional Institution dog training program, I've learned these and other lessons and I truly do believe that, as Sister Pauline told us the day she came to visit, the word "dog" is God spelled backward.

FORMERLY KNOWN AS STUBBY TAIL
Denise Mullard

"Whoever declared that love at first sight doesn't exist has never witnessed the purity of a puppy or looked deep into a puppy's eyes. If they did, their lives would change considerably."
— Elizabeth Parker

I'd done things the right way. I'd found a good job and stuck with it, married a wonderful man, and had a circle of family and friends. I was the one who could be counted on when people had a need.

I pictured myself working at least until I turned seventy. But there I was, only fifty-seven, forced to retire from a job I'd had for over thirty-five years.

Fibromyalgia and osteoarthritis were the two main diagnosis, but other medical problems also sucked the color and happiness out of my life. I'd always been a cheerful person, and the depression that settled over me was inescapable. Some days I barely got out of bed five minutes before my husband got home from work.

Even before my life fell apart and medical appointments and medications became my focus, we'd talked about getting a dog. My husband thought that was a great idea—but not until he retired. Dogs were a lot of work and so I agreed to wait.

There was no inciting incident, no one thing that made me wake up one morning determined to go to NEW PAWSibilities, a small independent rescue that was located a few miles away. I wasn't sure I'd adopt that day, but I was sinking deeper and deeper into depression, and I knew being alone while my husband was away was not working.

Their website was filled with dogs, each one cuter than the one before, and I read each bio wondering if this was the dog for me. I walked in nervous, with no idea of what I was doing. I had chosen a dog that seemed perfect. I knew nothing about the adoption process. I figured people there would guide me.

His name was Jim. I didn't know he was the owner when he walked into the welcome room wearing shorts, sandals, and a less that pristine t-shirt. When I mentioned the dog's name that interested me, Jim said I was too late; that particular dog had just been adopted.

It had taken a lot for me to get out of bed and make the trip, only to be disappointed. Maybe my husband was right. Maybe we should wait until he retired. As I turned to walk out the door and drive back to my empty life, Jim asked if maybe I would be interested in a puppy.

They had a litter of puppies that had been brought up from the high-kill shelter in Kentucky, where all of their dogs came from. These pups were so young they had not been posted online yet, so I would be able to see them first if I wanted.

"Yes, please!" I squealed. "I'd love to see them."

Jim walked me to a meet and greet room with toys and treats and left to get the dogs. I began second guessing myself. Was I up to a puppy? What would my husband say?

Jim returned, a puppy under each arm, and plopped the brothers onto the brightly colored rug. One walked all around the room first before finally coming over. The other one came straight to me and wanted to sit on my lap. My heart melted. For the first time in ages, a tiny bit of color seeped back into my life.

I spent some time visiting with the pups before telling Jim that I'd be back the next day with my husband Rick. I wasn't sure how he'd react, but I knew that, one way or another, one of those dogs was going home with me.

The next day we went back and Jim took us to the same room so Rick could meet the two puppies. As soon as Jim walked in with the dogs, I just knew the one I wanted. I had fallen in love with the cute little brown dog with the very short tail. Jim had explained that apparently the mama dog thought it was part of the umbilical cord and bit it off when he was born. Others might have been put off by the stumpy tail, but to me, it just added to his adorableness.

The puppies were too young to be away from their mama, but we put money down to hold him until he was ready to be adopted a few weeks later. The wait seemed interminable, but knowing we'd have a puppy to love filled me with hope. I had a reason to get out of bed again.

It had been a good twenty years since we had had a dog in the house, so it was quite an adventure starting out with a puppy again. We immediately went shopping for all everything we'd need to get him settled. It was fun choosing just the right collar and leash and figuring out what puppy food to buy. Then we added dishes, a bed, and toys to the cart.

Jim called my boy Stubby Tail but the name on his adoption papers was Mo. Rick is a big fan of The Zac Brown Band and so his official name is Zac The Brown Dog which soon became Zac.

We signed him up for puppy class—I'm proud to say that he passed with flying colors—and we even took him to a doggy swimming pool, which he loved.

I can't begin to tell you all the ways that adopting my sweet Zac changed my life. My body still hurts; I have moments of wondering why these medical challenges happened to me. But the joy of waking up to Zac each day gives me lots to look forward to. The doctors told me getting up and moving would help with the pain but, until Zac needed walking several times a day, I didn't see how moving would help. I guess the doctors were right, because it really does make a difference.

My circle had gotten smaller once I quit working and stayed in bed each day. But Zac is one of those dogs who loves greeting both two- and four-legged critters, and it's been fun getting to know new people because I go places. I even volunteered at fundraising and adoption events for NEW PAWSibilities.

I'm sure some people thought that adopting a puppy when I had physical ailments was a big mistake, but they were wrong. Sure, puppies need to go out in the middle of the night, they like to chew on things that don't belong to them, they want tons of attention. They might not be the best choice for people starting to wind down, but for me, Zac made life better in so many ways.

Zac will soon be eight years old and is slowing down a lot, as am I, but the love between us just keeps growing. During the past two years, we've rescued two more dogs from bad situations. Our house is full with three dogs and so is my heart. I love them all, but Zac will always be the most special; the one who rescued me.

MARLEY THE PUB DOG
Eileen Joyce Donovan

"Animal lovers are a special breed of humans, generous of spirit,
full of empathy, perhaps a little prone to sentimentality,
and with hearts as big as a cloudless sky"
— John Grogan

"We have company," my husband said, as I struggled to set up the perfect kindling pyramid base in the fireplace.

On my knees, I turned my head to look at him, but instead, found myself nose to nose with the biggest dog's face I had ever seen—easily twice the size of mine.

You've heard the phrase a gentle giant, and that is exactly what this dog was. He was well over 100 pounds; some people guessed he'd easily tip the scale at 140. We had no idea of his breed, but after perusing the various websites, we decided that his black, white, and rust coloring and markings were similar to a Swiss mountain dog, a large, heavy-boned breed with incredible physical strength.

"Well, hello," I said. He started licking my face with the same intensity as he wagged his tail.

"Where did you come from?" I asked between laughs.

"Remember those tracks we kept seeing? The ones with the paw prints and a straight line between them? They're from him. He had this chain hanging from his neck, tied on with this." My husband held up a long chain and a mess of plastic-coated wiring. "I can't believe he didn't get hung up on something, since he's been roaming around in our woods for a while."

"Can we keep him?"

"I'm not letting him go back to whoever did this to him. What do you want to call him?"

"Since it's Christmas Eve, and he came here all wrapped in chains, he has to be called Jacob Marley."

And just like that, Marley became a member of our family.

As I said, we had seen these strange tracks in the snow for days before Marley appeared. At the time, we owned a pub in the Adirondack Mountains, and even though many of our customers hunted, no one could identify the strange markings.

Thrilled to finally solve the mystery, we drove to the nearest mall to get a proper collar and leash, food and water bowls, food, treats, and toys. We rushed to get it all done before opening at noon for the lunch crowd.

As our customers trickled in, we asked everyone if they had seen Marley before or knew of someone whose dog had ran away. Not that we planned on giving him back, but we might report the person for animal abuse. No one had heard anything about a missing dog, but they all agreed he was a handsome animal.

Marley loved everyone and delighted in all the attention our customers showered upon him.

"It must have been the smells from the kitchen that kept him coming around," one customer said.

"Well, he'll never go hungry here," another one said.

Marley was an instant hit.

Since we lived in the woods, we opened the door every morning and let him roam the forest alone or with his woodland friends, until he felt like coming home. Often the two dogs across the road would join him on these morning outings.

To show us just how grateful he was, he started bringing home "gifts" from his morning romps. These gifts varied from an old, beat-up squeaky toy, to a two-gallon, insulated water jug, to a fairly new ski boot (just one), and an assortment of items left on porches or in back yards.

We began to worry about how our neighbors would react to this, so we made sure everyone knew what Marley had appropriated so it could be returned to its rightful owner. But no one ever claimed anything.

I always thought the most interesting "thank you" he brought home happened one day when I saw him trotting up the driveway, his jaws opened to an almost impossible, degree. Gently clutched in the giant's jaws were two large rolls, still warm from the oven. Amazingly, there were no dent marks on those soft, buttery mounds. To this day, I can't figure out how he accomplished that feat. I opened the door to let him in and, tail wagging furiously, he dropped the yeasty bread at my feet,

"Some woman is going to spend her morning wondering where her rolls disappeared to and cursing the thief," I said to my husband.

"Probably. But we'll never hear about it."

"No, I guess not. No one ever seems to hear anyone complaining about stolen items."

"He's becoming a master thief," my husband said, giving Marley another bone-shaped biscuit while secretly tossing the still-warm rolls in the trash can.

Fortunately, before the village, or the surrounding villages, came looking for us with torches lit, pitchforks in hand, and demands of reparations for stolen goods, Marley decided he had done enough to show us how thankful he was for adopting him, and stopped the gift giving.

Our regular customers were disappointed. It had become a bit of a game to guess what Marley brought home from his morning excursions every day.

Marley, our gentle giant, became a fixture in the pub. Customers brought their dogs to play with him, little children rode on his back and pretended he was a pony, and everyone thought he was the best dog they ever met.

And he was.

MEANT TO BE MURDOCK
Gerald Hendrickson

"How can anyone abandon a beautifully loyal dog?
It's not an accessory, it's your best friend."
— Ricky Gervais

Oh, my God; he's going to die before my very eyes!

Those thoughts that ran through my head as I witnessed a frightened dog running in the middle of a busy street. Cars were swerving to avoid running him over. Not thinking clearly about my own safety, I spun my car across the middle of the street in the hope of blocking oncoming traffic and sparing this little dog.

Just moments earlier as I was driving home from work, the most important item on my agenda was what I would be preparing for dinner that night. Little did I realize how much my life would change in the next few seconds.

I jumped out of my car and ran to the little dog that was still in the street.

He'll never let me get close to him, I thought as I saw the little cream and tan pooch shaking with fright.

Convinced that he was going to run if I got any closer, I saw the collar and figured that the owner's name and phone number would be there. If I could only grab the pooch or the collar, I'd have a chance to reunite the probably frantic owner with his or her dog.

I was wrong on both counts. He happily allowed me to scoop him up, and I settled him on my lap once got into the car. I'll never forget the trusting gaze he gave me. That look of pure unadulterated love opened up something in my soul I hadn't known was closed off. It was as though I was his hero, and he was claiming me to be his master from now on. And the I.D. tag? It was conspicuously absent.

With no easy way to find the owner, I started getting nervous. I decided to drive up and down the side streets asking anyone I saw if they knew where he belonged.

No one recognized him. I reluctantly decided to take him home for the night.

We already have two dogs, so a third one was out of the question for us. We called the police and Humane Society to report him, but there was no record of a missing dog that matched his description. We went on numerous social media platforms and provided pictures of him, but no one stepped forward. It looked like I was going to be his foster dad until I could find a good home for him.

He was filthy and hungry. I gave him a bath, cleaned him up, and gave him food, which he practically inhaled. He followed me everywhere. As long as he knew I was nearby, he was a happy dog.

To my anger and dismay, I discovered that someone had severed his vocal cords, making him incapable of barking. His only way to communicate was through pitiful squeaking sounds. He was not house or kennel trained. Each morning when I came downstairs to retrieve him from his kennel, I found him standing in his own filth.

I decided to name him Murdock, after the street where I found him. I'm a chiropractor and decided to take him to my office during the day. The patients fell in love with him, taking turns holding him in the waiting room. They brought him toys, treats, even a dog bed for him to sleep in when he was at the office. He loved the attention, and it was therapeutic for the patients, especially the elderly, to interact with this loving little dog.

I ramped up my efforts to adopt him out. Several potential families expressed great interest in him. All promised they'd adopt him and give him a good home. In the end, however, they all reconsidered their earlier decision.

Gradually, however, something magical happened. I began to develop a learning curve with Murdock. I was able to successfully kennel train him. He was given some liberties to roam about the house with fewer and fewer accidents.

The other two dogs accepted and developed a relationship with him. Of course the biggest and most important plus is that my wife fell in love with him. She began to lobby on his behalf for us to adopt Murdock. As the learning curve continued, we got into a groove, a rhythm. It got easier to care for him. He became a part of our family.

I finally came to the conclusion that he had captured all of our hearts, and he was now a member of our family. You can't give a family member away, after all, can you? So Murdock belongs to us, finally. I may have saved his life that day on Murdock Street, but Murdock has, in turn, enriched our lives with the unconditional love that he has brought to us.

CHAPTER SIX

BIRD OF PARADISE
TRANSFORMATION

THE COURAGE TO GROW

"We may think we are nurturing our garden,
but of course it's our garden that is really nurturing us."
– Jenny Uglow

Over 35 years ago I went to a Liberty House to shop for a wedding gift. It was a top-tier store that I could only afford when there were special sales.

I ended up in the housewares department and spied a pitcher with a magnificent bird of paradise design. I had recently gotten divorced and could not afford it, so I kept browsing and found a more budget-friendly gift. The bride loved whatever I got her—I seriously don't remember what I bought—and that was that.

Except it wasn't. I went back to the second floor more than once to gaze on that beautiful piece that somehow spoke to me. As a single mom paying off an expensive divorce attorney, I should not have kept dreaming of owning the pottery.

One day I went to buy shoes for my boys from the final markdown shoe rack. I went back to the housewares and fancy gifts section and saw that there was only one pitcher left and it was discounted by twenty-five percent. I whipped out my red Liberty House credit card with the yellow hibiscus and bought it as a gift for myself.

In 1996, we moved to Florida because my new husband had a terminal brain disease, and I thought there would be better and more affordable healthcare. Big mistake. I sold most of our belongings, but I kept the pitcher and a few other Hawaii memories.

After he died, I remarried. We moved back to Kailua in 2005, and along came my one piece of bird of paradise pottery. I truly thought I'd never leave Hawaii again except for vacations. You guessed it; wrong again. My 2015 traumatic brain injury and severe concussion got to be too much for me to work with people as a concierge, and so, once again, in 2017, we sold and gave away most of our belongings, shipped what we thought we could not live without, and relocated to Wisconsin.

A few treasures from Hawaii made the trip including the bird of paradise pottery. I've packed and unpacked this piece more times than I care to remember, and I love it more now than ever.

Maybe it spoke to me because the bird of paradise's vivid and stunning appearance is a metaphor for individual transformation. The flower serves as a reminder to let go of the past and to transform ourselves, to discover new things, and grow personally.

I think Coconut was a runner who never reconnected with his first family down in Kentucky. When we first got him, he inhaled his food to the point where it seemed he would choke, and he didn't like being touched. I look back at the dog we adopted, and he is not at all the one we have today. Truly this pup of mine has been transformed through a combination of love, patience, time, and training. And aren't those the same things we need to transform ourselves?

Every flower featured in this book, except for the bird of paradise, is one that we planted and nurtured ourselves. I went back and forth about including an exotic tropical bloom, but decided to because much of my life and transformation happened in Hawaii.

There are still many months before the first spring flowers bloom. But when they finally do, I'll fill my pitcher with daffodils and tulips from my yard. In the summer and fall, it will hold every flower mentioned in these pages and even more.

I don't know what gave me the courage to buy a vase I could not afford or to move all those times to and from Hawaii. But I am glad to have this reminder of the grace and beauty of Hawaii. I would have never adopted a dog had it not been for all the many steps on my journey to being transformed into the me I am today.

A CHANCE TO LOVE
Diane Smits

"Adopting a shelter dog is an excellent way to turn love into action. The love you receive is an extraordinary extra benefit."
— Abby Underdog

My in-laws, Lee and Bette, had always had a dog in their lives. Their last dog, Dallas, passed away at the ripe old age of fourteen a few years back. Dallas was a poodle/mix who travelled everywhere with them. Each winter they'd make the trip to Tennessee with Dallas to spend the winter with their daughter, Amy.

The years went by, and Bette's health deteriorated to the point where living at home was no longer an option. Lee stayed in their house with his memories when his wife moved to the nursing home.

My husband and I lived right next door, but we had two active teens and our full-time jobs, so we didn't alleviate Lee's loneliness much. Lee had always been active with a variety of interests. Besides being a talented artist, he played golf and pool and was always eager to spend time with family and friends.

As his circle of friends passed away or they weren't physically able to do all they used to do, we noticed Lee was becoming lonely and depressed. We wondered how to include him more or to help him find new ways to spend time. We realized that he needed a companion.

Our Boston terrier, Eli, loved playing with him, and Lee was a wonderful dog sitter when we went out of town. We talked to him and decided to find Lee an older dog, a dog that would be content to sit on his lap, a dog that needed love and companionship like Lee did.

So, our journey began. I checked newspaper ads and spent hours checking Petfinder and similar sites. Finding nothing that would work, I expanded my search to shelters within driving distance looking for the perfect match.

Not wanting Lee to get excited only to have someone adopt a dog before he got approved, I'd submit the application without telling him. The first couple of times his application was rejected, I didn't connect the dots. By the fourth or fifth time I got the sinking feeling his age was a factor. I could have lied and filled out the applications with all my information, but that would not be right, and the dog needed to be a good fit for Lee, so the search continued.

Spring blended into summer with no luck. I was ready to give up but over the fourth of July weekend I found a Boston terrier at an independent rescue in Oshkosh. I called NEW PAWSibilities, hoping that they were open and that anyone else interested in the dog would be too busy with parades, cookouts, and fireworks to call.

Not only were they open, but the dog was still there. I explained that Lee was probably not the youngest person who would be interested in adopting but that he was healthy, active, and needed a companion. They weren't concerned about Lee's age, and they encouraged us to bring our dog along for the meet and greet.

We set off excited at the prospect of finally finding a rescue shelter that wouldn't hold Lee's age against him. For the first time in months, there was hope.

We learned that Valborg, yes, that was his name, had come into the shelter with two other Boston terriers. They had been surrendered because the owner had been incarcerated on drug charges.

The dogs had been neglected in her care, sometimes being left alone inside for days without food and water. A relative took in the dogs for a while, but then surrendered the trio to the rescue.

Valborg came running into the room right to Lee. We immediately knew two things: there was going to be a name change, and it was love at first sight.

My heart melted, and I'll admit to a few tears in the meeting room. It was like this wonderful pooch knew Lee needed him. The whole visit could not have been more perfect. Red, a much better name than Valborg, played with all of us and the two dogs frolicked outside; it was obvious they would be great friends.

We went for a walk to make sure Lee could handle him. Red was a perfect gentleman. These two were obviously meant for each other, so we filled out the application.

With it being a holiday weekend we were prepared to wait for their decision. We figured we would be first in line if anyone else was interested, but the thought of leaving Red there was hard. The adoption counselor left us in the room with Red and came back a short while later with great news.

Red was ours as soon as we paid the fee and went over the adoption contract. I had not seen such a huge smile on Lee's face for quite some time. A part of me was worried that they might change their mind because everyone else seemed to think that Lee was too old for dog. We told the adoption counselor one last time that we lived right next door and checked on Lee every day. Of course, we reminded him that Red would also have Eli as a playmate.

With a smile almost as big as Lee's, the counselor assured us that they had no reservations at all and sent us on our way with well wishes for a happy future.

Red was a great dog with a few quirks. Whenever he saw fly swatters, long sticks, or rolled up newspapers he would attack them, leading us to believe he was probably beaten. Lee had a pool table in his house, and there was a learning curve with those cues.

Red played well with other dogs and loved any person he met. He had the occasional accident in the house if Lee didn't read his signs properly, but it didn't take long to figure things out. Given the situation he came out of he could have had many more severe problems, but he did not.

Lee and Red were inseparable and had many wonderful adventures. They were a familiar sight throughout the neighborhood. Whether it was a visit to see Bette in the nursing home, a quick trip to the store, a long walk down the driveway to get the mail, a golf cart ride through the woods, or a trip to winter in Tennessee, Red was Lee's ever-present companion.

After Bette passed away, Lee needed nursing home care. We were now empty-nesters and had added another Boston Terrier to our family. We welcomed Red into our home for the rest of his days. Lee and Red have since passed on, but we are comforted knowing that Lee, Bette, and Red are together.

Seniors still have a lot of love to give and our family will always be grateful to NEW PAWSibilities for giving an old man the best dog who gave him love and companionship when they both needed it the most.

AND THEN I GOT A DOG

"Be the person your dog thinks you are."
— C.J. Frick

I recorded a podcast earlier this year called Un-caped Heroes. The show's concept is that heroes are out there who don't wear capes and don't leap over buildings in a single bound. The host interviews people who do things others think are amazing. These are regular people who stumbled into what has become their mission.

The host and I had a conversation about my not being a dog person, about my journey to adopting Coconut, and about what a profound impact he has had on me. My volunteering started as a way to thank Coconut for saving my life and because everyone needs a purpose.

Most people in the animal wellness field are great with animals, but not so much with marketing. I happened to be just the opposite. I started writing doggy bios for the website. After that I redesigned the animal rescue shelter's logo, created a new website, managed their Facebook page, wrote grants, and started doing events. Getting that involved with them was not intentional, but I know I made a difference.

I love doing podcasts because it's a great way to share how everyone can do something to help animals in need. During the ten years NEW PAWSibilities was open, they rescued over 12,000 dogs from a high-kill shelter in Kentucky. During the four years I helped, before and during COVID-19, I wrote bios and helped to find homes for more than 6,500 of those dogs.

When the host heard those numbers, she called me a hero, a title I don't deserve. All I wanted to do was to find a way to add meaning to my life which, when you think about it, is pretty self-serving.

People think I write books, donate money, and create awareness about the many problems surrounding homeless canines because I am an animal activist. Trust me, they could not be more wrong when pinning that label on me

Whatever I do in the animal wellness area is for people like me. There are suicidal women who need a dog to save their lives. The list of lonely, broken people who need a special friend with four paws is endless. They include families with autistic children, seniors who have given up on life due to health challenges, veterans with PTSD, and so many others.

During our time together, I was finally able to articulate why I continue writing about rescue dogs. Most people don't need a purebred or a designer breed. That is the most expensive way to obtain a best friend. That's not to say there aren't people who have good reasons and the resources to have a specific breed. I am not anti-breeding as long as it's done in an ethical and humane manner. Paying hundreds and even thousands of dollars, plus the added costs of spay/neuter surgery and all of the vaccinations, is beyond what the average person can afford.

I know the life-saving value of a mutt. When I was at my lowest and suicide was a very real option, I could not afford a purebred no matter how beneficial a canine might have been.

When there's no money to pay the vet for spay/neuter surgery or to transport dogs to a place without a stray dog population, then we as a nation will continue to kill dogs because they are an inconvenience. Each dog that is euthanized because of an overcrowded shelter is one less dog that can change a person's life. For a fraction of the cost of buying from a breeder, people can afford to adopt a dog that has already been fixed, has up-to-date vaccinations, and is ready to love and be loved.

I write and speak about these issues because I believe we live in an increasingly unkind world. Every rescue dog has the power to give their person hope and to bring them joy.

Moving from Hawaii to Oshkosh was harder than I ever imagined. And then I got a dog. And then I found a purpose. And now I have a life. And, along the way, I made a difference. I still say I'm not a hero, but I am grateful for the twists and turns that helped me play even a small role in saving thousands of dogs and to help create new families in the process.

A THERAPY DOG WASHOUT
Janet Charbonneau

"The face of a golden retriever feels like home."
— David Rosenfelt

In 2015, I hiked 440 miles over the Camino de Santiago in northern Spain. I have done many interesting things in my life, but this hike in celebration of my fiftieth birthday was the hardest I'd have ever done. Not only was I celebrating a huge milestone birthday, but I was also out there to help me get out of a rut and to learn how to take chances again.

After a divorce and loss of a job, I had lost all confidence in relationships and commitment. My commitment fears were not only about finding love again but also in committing to owning another dog.

While I was hiking the Camino, we ran across a beautiful golden retriever. I had owned two goldens in the past, and I desperately wanted another one. But I was afraid something would happen, and I would not be able to afford to take care of one.

My fears were warranted, my having been on unemployment for a year after losing my job. I'd had a successful IT career before leaving my job, moving onto a sailboat, and being semi-retired. Going back to work was harder than I had imagined. After some false starts, I finally had started a promising IT job, but the fear still gripped me.

People who have hiked the Camino will tell you that they were changed in many ways. I'm no different. One of the biggest and best takeaways was realizing that I wanted to own a dog again.

Shortly after my return, I reached out to several golden retriever rescue groups including the Grateful Goldens Rescue of the Lowcountry. The coordinator contacted me about a dog named Holly that they were bringing with others to a festival in Florence, S.C. one Saturday when I wasn't working. I decided to go and meet her.

I had wanted a golden that I could train to be a therapy dog. Holly was five years old and so ridiculously shy that I didn't know if she would break out of her shell to be friendly around people. That's a big requirement for therapy dogs. Still, there was something about her, so I took a chance and fostered her with the agreement that, if it did not work out, they would find another forever home for her.

When I got her to my house, she was so timid I wondered if she had been abused. She had been rescued from a house in Myrtle Beach where she had been a breeder's dog, along with her sister and another golden. The breeder had moved upstate and left his three dogs behind. His neighbor reached out to a rescue organization to save them. Poor Holly had just had a litter of puppies who were no longer with her. Ripped away from her puppies and her sister, she was fragile and devastated.

During the first couple of days of fostering, I had to open the door to the backyard and step away because she didn't want to be anywhere near me. After a couple of days, she finally let me pet her and gave me a goldie smile. After two months of fostering, I knew she would not make a good therapy dog. But I was hooked and couldn't imagine putting her into another unknown situation, so I adopted her.

It took a couple of years for her to become more comfortable around people. She gradually started to trust me—very slowly, but surely.

In March 2020, my mother passed away, just as the COVID–19 shutdown was starting. I couldn't even be in the hospital with her on her last couple of days, as the hospital would only let one relative stay with her till the end. I spent a couple of months cleaning out my mother's house. I was devastated, and I could tell that Holly missed her gram as much as I did.

A couple times a week my sister would come over to help clean Mom's house, and we would end our day on the front porch for happy hour and wonderful chats. The time came when I moved back to my house in Charleston. I was working from home, as was everyone else, and wasn't seeing any of my friends or coworkers. It was just Holly and me.

I know I would not have survived that time without Holly. She absolutely saved me, as I had saved her five years earlier. As Holly and I kept each other company during that crazy lockdown time, I realized I could not stay in Charleston and survive. I had to move to be closer to my family. In November of 2020, as the country started to open up again, I rented a house outside of Raleigh, because my entire family lived in North Carolina.

It took me several months to prepare and sell my property in Charleston, so we traveled back and forth between houses. However, I was able to spend some wonderful, quality time with my sister, Lois, who helped me survive the pandemic. In July 2021, Holly and I became residents of the tar heel state.

I built a new house, and Holly and I moved there in September 2022. I cleaned out pine trees, then sodded and mulched the back yard, after installing a new fence for Holly. At twelve years old, she still adores rolling in the grass and now has plenty of that to roll in. She loves the backyard that I designed for her.

This wonderful therapy dog washout has brought such joy to my life. One of her favorite things to do is to lie on her back for a tummy rub with a silly, goofy grin showing off her fangs. She knows this will make me laugh, and I will give her that tummy rub. Many mornings I wake up to her expression, and I burst out laughing and immediately get up. There is no better way to start a day.

Hiking the Camino de Santiago gave me a confidence that I desperately needed and prepared me for so many bumps in the road I could never have predicted. But, without a doubt, the best thing about that trip was realizing that it was time to get a dog.

During COVID–19, I worked from home with no outside contact, except for a masked grocery-shopping trip every couple of weeks. Like others, I was barely in survival mode. Holly kept me sane. I love this precious girl and am so happy that we rescued each other.

THE SKINNY DOG I NEVER KNEW I NEEDED
Stevie Anderson

"Every human should not buy a dog but rescue in need and free
him from the sufferings and give him love, care, and shelter."
— Ridhima Badola

By the time I'd reached my sixties, my two young adult sons' three childhood puppies were in their elder years. I loved those dogs, but now that I was working from home at my remote job, it seemed the perfect time for a puppy. I knew this would likely be my last dog and that puppies take time and can be a handful. Still, I was excited to have one of my very own.

A friend of a friend bred Chihuahuas, and that's where I found Lucy, who made my life perfectly complete. Together we enjoyed puppy obedience sessions, followed by agility classes. Lucy became my constant companion.

One of the older dogs passed around that time, and while it's sad saying goodbye, I decided that three dogs would be my limit. As we were settling into our happy lives, a friend asked if I'd go with her to pick up her puppy from a new rescue group in our state.

Little Charlotte's Rescue brings stray dogs from the south of Texas up to Wisconsin. When I joined my friend to pick up the new pup, I was impressed by the love these people had for the dogs and how they volunteered to help in any way they could.

I learned that a big need was for foster families. I decided to foster, if it meant saving the lives of dogs that would otherwise be left behind. We met the transport, and I spent the next couple of hours walking the bigger adult dogs who were waiting for their foster families to arrive.

When the last pup I was babysitting got picked up, I headed to the puppy area. A strange, deer-type creature bounded across the yard. I had never seen a dog that looked like that, and I wondered what it was. Laughing, I sat down, and this strange creature trotted over and draped her long neck over mine.

I was delighted when I learned she was one of the pups who needed a foster, and immediately offered to take her. Her name was Betty Boop, and she was the skinniest creature I'd ever seen.

I took her home and started calling her BB. If ever a girl needed weight, it was BB, but she wouldn't eat. My other foster pup made himself at home immediately, but this new girl only wanted to be as close to me as possible at all times.

I wasn't worried the first day, understanding that she was obviously very stressed and scared. By the evening of day two, I contacted Cheri, the director of the rescue. I explained that I had tried baby food, hot dogs, cheese, and bone broth. Nothing tempted her. Cheri reminded me about The Rule of Three, also called 3–3–3.

The first three days are the hardest for any dog, where everything is new and different. By week three, they start becoming aware of the household routine and their true personality begins to emerge. Around the third month, they understand this is their forever home. There might be some behavioral quirks to work out, but the adjustment period is over.

Once I remembered the Rule of Three, I felt better, but BB still refused to eat. The next morning I put a chicken in to roast, thinking the delicious aroma would entice her. I pulled it out of the oven, cut off a small piece, blew on it a bit to cool it, and offered it to her. She looked at me sadly and turned away.

I messaged Cheri and told her that if I could get this dog to eat, I had to keep her.

"Stevie, she will eat by tomorrow," came her response.

Easy for her to say. She wasn't there to see my every offering rebuffed.

"I mean it. Shall I come down now and sign the adoption papers?"

I guess that's when I knew BB was mine. I went back to the kitchen to strip the chicken carcass and get it into the fridge.

As usual, BB was on my feet. I accidentally dropped a piece of chicken and she gobbled it down. I gave her another, and she ate it. I couldn't believe my eyes. A part of me knew that this little dog had just waited until I gave her a sign of some sort and that she had played me like that proverbial fiddle. Or maybe, just maybe, that was the moment she began to trust me, because she sensed my commitment. Either way, she was home.

My son's girlfriend met BB that afternoon and asked where I had gotten the baby kangaroo. Something clicked, and I knew that her name was Joey, since that's what they call a baby kangaroo in the land down under.

I thought I had wanted one last puppy, but Joey has enriched my life in ways I could never have imagined. The opportunity to volunteer for a rescue that encourages and supports their volunteers, fosters, and transport drivers is now a large part of my life.

I've been able to go on a transport, something I had never considered, and I fostered a mom and her pups for eight weeks. I get to play with and watch wonderful canines coming up from deplorable conditions in south Texas. The foster program eventually allows these dogs to become much-loved family members here in Wisconsin.

I cannot imagine my life without Joey, and she is the perfect Texas cousin to our fosters. She welcomes them and lets them in on all the tricks to winning the hearts of their new families.

I thought life was perfect with three dogs. It improved exponentially with the addition of the skinny dog I never knew I needed.

MY REPURPOSED LIFE

"I have found that when you are deeply troubled,
there are things you get from the silent devoted companionship
of a dog that you can get from no other source."
– Doris Day

One day, the following words popped up as a memory on my social media page:

"I wonder if people who commit suicide have regrets in heaven?"

I read my thoughts from eight years ago and was immediately transported to that desperate time when I truly believed that suicide was my only option.

What had started as a simple trip home from the beach ended in a five-car pileup started by an uninsured, inattentive driver while we sat waiting at a red light. Our small car, sandwiched between two SUVs, was totaled. My husband, who was driving, suffered no injuries.

I don't know if my head hit the phone I was holding or if it was the other way around. Either way, those few seconds resulted in blunt force trauma from the impact, leaving a hole in my brain. I suffered a concussion from the whiplash, moderate frontal and temporal brain damage, and a level-ten migraine. I've had a headache every day since.

My doctor explained that I would have to learn to manage the resulting depression, anxiety, and suicidal thoughts while my brain healed. He suggested that an emotional support dog would make a big difference. I told him no. A few months passed, and he brought it up a second time during an appointment. Again I refused.

I struggled to keep up the happy façade, but when I wasn't working as a concierge at the upscale Waikiki Beach hotel, I was plotting my death. After eighteen months the struggle became too much, and I put in my two-week notice.

Without my income, we could no longer afford to live in paradise. In March of 2017, we moved from sunny Hawaii to cold, gloomy Oshkosh. Leaving a life I loved and starting over at age sixty-two was much harder than I expected. Besides my son, his wife, and their son, we didn't know anyone and knew nothing about our new community.

One day in July, while my husband was working thirty miles away in Appleton, I decided to walk downtown and explore. The deafening noise of a flyover from EAA Air Adventure, something I had known nothing about before that day, resulted in instantaneous pain from the noise-induced migraine.

The pain was like a red-hot poker relentlessly being stabbed into my forehead. Unable to stand when the shaking made my legs wobbly, I sat in the middle of the sidewalk in front of the post office and sobbed. My brain was so broken that I thought there were Nazi planes overhead, and I was in blitz-ravaged London.

I sat on the summer-hot pavement, and no one stopped or asked me if I was okay. No one called the police. People walked around me as quickly as possible. When I was all cried out, I walked home to my empty house.

After the wreck I bought a set of knives, ostensibly for cooking, but that was not the reason. I had thought about pills, and every day I researched how many of each prescription drug I was on would I need to take to die. Using a sharp knife seemed so much easier.

The movers lost, broke, or stole most of what we had carefully decided to ship to Wisconsin to start our new lives. One of the missing boxes held the nearly new knives. My mind raced as I tried to come up with a plan because life truly was not worth living. I remember thinking that people in Oshkosh cared more about their dogs than they did about each other.

That was the moment I knew I did not trust myself to be alone. In over two years nothing else I had tried had taken away the pain, the anxiety, or the deep, overwhelming sadness; I'd try a dog. If it didn't help, at least my canine-loving husband would have a friend when I killed myself.

It took a few months of convincing myself that a dog would make a difference, but in October of that first year, we went to a rescue shelter to start the process. Gary tried and failed to hide his excitement about finally getting a dog. Every dog he thought would be fun went straight to him. They all ignored me. Finally I suggested that if the dog was supposed to be my emotional support dog, it might help if it had even a modicum of interest in me.

After a discussion with us about the kind of dog that might be a good fit, Jim, the owner of the rescue we'd found online, left the room and came back with an underweight fourteen-month-old brown pooch with a long black tail. He was of indeterminate breed and, for some reason, came directly to me and sat staring as if to say he had made his choice. He had been there for three weeks and not one person had ever asked to see him. I'm not sure why, but there was obviously a connection, and we went home with the dog that saved my life.

I made mistakes as a dog owner. Lots of mistakes. Costly ones. I can laugh now, but it was a wild first few months.

My big turnaround came when I found a purpose. The rescue desperately needed marketing support which happened to be my strength. During the four years I helped them before they became a COVID–19 casualty, I rebranded and redesigned their website, wrote grants, created events, and pretty much became the face of the rescue.

The thing about getting a dog is no matter life's twists and turns, I have a partner on the journey who will never disappoint me. The miracle of his rescue and transport from Kentucky to Wisconsin still amazes me. It's as if he specifically came to this one rescue shelter to save my life. And I moved all the way from Hawaii, kicking and screaming, to save his.

Coconut forced me to get outside, and those regular walks improved my fitness and my attitude. Walking him helped me to meet my neighbors since dogs are people magnets. When humans see someone in pain, they want try and come up with a fix. But dogs aren't like that; they help us to see that not all problems can be fixed or, if they can be, it's not usually an overnight solution.

That first Christmas, Jim gave me a gift card, and I bought a little orange dog made from a repurposed piece of metal. The true gift was the note he scribbled on a torn piece of yellow note paper.

"Thank you for being my light. You have brought me and our staff out of the darkness. You are my friend, my sister, and my fantastic queen of everything. Thank you so much."

I still miss my old life in Hawaii. I'll probably never be headache-free. Coconut, the dog no one else wanted, has helped me to live in the present, to find joy in the most unexpected places, and to find purpose in my life.

My orange metal dog reminds me every day to give myself time to heal and to accept that I am no longer the me I was. Coconut never met the old Carmen. He loves this Carmen more than any person in his world. I guess that's all that matters.

ONE DAY AT A TIME
Rosie Maureen as told by Joyce Bean Leeman

*"Being a hero to someone, even if it is just a dog, is a feeling
like no other. Though it can be frustrating, it can be the most
rewarding thing to give someone a second chance at life."*
— Elizabeth Parker

A few years ago, my neighbor Joyce retired after working at a government job for three decades. She spent countless hours volunteering at a local food bank. Knowing there were so many needs, she and her daughter Andrea opened another food bank in the United Methodist church and spent hours helping the members and others in their community.

Joyce had a busy life filled with visits with her three daughters, seven grandchildren, and six great-grandchildren. Any leftover time was spent reading, swimming, and relaxing at her local library or bookstore.

Still, when she returned to her home each night, the house seemed a bit too quiet. She had a large tabby cat named Ginger, but she missed the pleasure of owning a dog, since her furry companion had departed a few years earlier.

At 72 years of age, she pondered if it would be fair to adopt a dog that might outlive her. Was it right to have her children take on the responsibility of a pet they might not want or have time for when she passed?

Things sometimes have a way of working out the way they were meant to and that's exactly what happened this time. An acquaintance of a friend's friend owned an Australian shepherd named Lucy who needed a home.

Once the puppy had outgrown its cuteness and grew larger, the family placed her in a cage when they went to work. Lucy was solidly built at about twenty-three inches high and weighed sixty pounds, so the cost of feeding her was also a factor. At under a year, she was still a puppy, albeit a big one. Lucy spent most of her time caged or locked in a garage, causing her to withdraw and become anti-social.

Joyce was a lifelong animal advocate. Once she learned about Lucy, she knew something had to be done. Her plan was to meet her and then to spread the word and somehow find the girl a home. And then she met that big, beautiful pooch.

Lucy was gorgeous with a slightly wavy, lush, medium-length coat. She had feathering on the back of her legs and a generous mane around her neck. The classic tricolor coat with white markings was only one of her standout features. Her remarkable enormous and piercing amber eyes followed Joyce's every step. Without hesitation, Joyce decided she would rescue Lucy.

When they got home Joyce realized that Lucy was more than shy; she was traumatized. Joyce fell back into her workplace habit and began researching what to do to help a traumatized dog. She learned that Australian shepherds are not the kind of dogs to lie around the living room all day or live happily in a crate with only a fifteen-minute walk. They are an intense breed that must have a great deal of exercise and something to occupy their mind each day. If not, they become bored, which usually leads to serious behavior problems. Without enough mental and physical exercise, they can become nervous when left alone.

Lucy had been mishandled in her youth, which had left her cowering as she tried to avoid contact. Her breed was also prone to running away. Although physically much larger, Lucy was even afraid of Joyce's cat.

Joyce updated Lucy's shots and took her to the groomer and local parks. Together Lucy and her rescuer shared long hikes and meals at regular times. If Joyce needed to be away from home a longer time, she would leave a "special" toy for Lucy to chew on and a small treat.

She encouraged Lucy to relax during their alone time and made sure not to never punish her by locking her away.

She placed a basket with various size balls, chewing ropes and elaborate dog toys in the living room. After about six months of Joyce working with her each day, Lucy gradually learned to trust her. Within a year Lucy even bonded with Ginger the cat.

Years passed and this courageous dog became a good watchdog for Joyce's home. Lucy even scared a California brown bear from the trash cans and chased a stray dog out of their yard.

One afternoon Joyce fell in her bathroom. Joyce's friend Kimmy called an ambulance, but the real hero was Lucy. Thanks to her frantic barking, someone realized that Joyce needed help. The faithful canine was waiting with an always-wagging tail when Joyce returned home from the hospital.

The duo have been together for almost ten years. Joyce is now eighty-two and Lucy is happily living her best life. It's a joy to see her becoming more easygoing each day, remaining puppy-like even in her senior years.

It takes a special person to disrupt his or her retirement plans and adopt a dog others would write off. Joyce says no one can predict the future, and she doesn't know how long either she or her Lucy will be on this earth. She does know that she will keep on loving Lucy one day at a time.

BROKEN ISN'T USELESS

"Everything has beauty, but not everyone sees it."
— Confucius

I never set out to have a house full of stained-glass, though I've always loved it. We started with matching Tiffany-style lamps for our bedroom that we bought from a local antique mall. Then two became four, and it seemed that whenever I needed a lamp to banish the gloom from our north facing home, a term I had never heard until it was too late, I'd find another one until I ended up with ten. And the foyer ceiling fixture brings the grand total to eleven.

Next, I discovered a gorgeous stained-glass room divider to block the view of the ugly house next door. That led to a window medallion in my office. The dining room windows across the way seemed lacking, so the hunt was on for two more medallions.

A few years ago, we had window cleaners in for the second time ever because, at a certain age, people and ladders to reach the second-floor exterior windows aren't a good match. Instead of drilling holes into the brand-new window frames, Gary used a large suction hook to display the fragile medallions.

Gary used a large suction hook to display the fragile medallions. The workers carefully placed the stained-glass pieces on the table, removed the suction cups, cleaned the windows, and, when the windows were dry, put everything back, and continued working elsewhere. Within minutes of their leaving, I heard an ominous crash. The suction had not held on one of the windows and we walked in and saw a sea of colored glass littering the floor.

My friend had owned this house before we had bought it from her. We connected in a roundabout way a year after we both moved. That random online meeting has been a blessing in our lives—including the fact that her mother creates and repairs stained glass.

Angie carted the broken pieces to Milwaukee, and her mother assured me they would be better than new when she was done. I just didn't know it would take eight months. Every time I passed the now-naked windows I lamented their emptiness. They were purchased online, and I had lots of credit card points given all my pandemic shopping, so I bought two more. A part of me doubted the first two would ever find their way back to Oshkosh. Oh, me of little faith.

I've never enjoyed being wrong more than the moment when I saw the repaired medallions looking, as her mom had promised, better than new. We took the newer pair and hung them in the kitchen. A few weeks later, one crashed to the floor. Don't worry, there's a happy ending.

We finally screwed hooks into the brand-new vinyl windows, something I had been against from the start, bought new chains as the others had been shortened, bought sunflower medallions for the kitchen—credit card points to the rescue again—and placed the orphaned two on top of the refrigerator. I didn't have the nerve to ask Angie's mom to repair the newly-broken medallions so, there they sat gathering dust.

When our rain garden started showing off last year, I shopped for yard art things to liven up the new garage siding. I'm not sure what sparked the idea, but I ordered two ninety-six-inch shepherd hooks. I even paid for them without points, and added them to the colorful flowers and native grasses.

Broken doesn't mean useless. My life is filled with broken people, broken dogs, and, now, broken glass. My traumatic brain injury sure qualifies me as broken.

I used to work with a rescue helping to find homes for dogs from a high-kill shelter. Some of the animals had been abused, abandoned, left for broken or dead. With love, training, medical care, and time dogs that people think are broken become special and much-loved companions.

Stained glass artists create beauty from shattered pieces and turn them into new and even improved works of art. My garden glass isn't perfect, but on a sunny day with light reflecting off the multi-hued brilliance, my rescue glass has never looked more special. When I see my rescue dog zooming throughout the garden under one of the dazzling medallions I smile, grateful for all the beauty in my yard.

HOBIE'S HALF-WAY HOUSE
Ellie Ray Spivey

"The greatest fear dogs know is the fear that you will not come back when you go out the door without them."
— Stanley Coren

As I was being dragged across the shelter parking lot by my newly adopted cocker spaniel, I began to wonder if I had bitten off more than I could chew. *Can I handle this dog? Is he too much energy for me?*

I struggled to untangle the leash around my legs as the volunteer yelled, "Oh yeah, forgot to tell you that Hobie only walks in circles!"

"Thanks for the heads up," I replied, as I questioned my decision again.

Later, as we began to settle in, belly rubs, long naps, and, of course, walking in circles, became our normal routine. My affection for this crazy boy grew rapidly. All was going well with our relationship until disaster struck.

After a long day of volunteering in a nearby pre-school, I returned home to find my living room filled with shredded drapes, pillow stuffing, and gnawed shoes. My oriental rug was no more, and my $400 eyeglasses were on the floor in too many pieces to repair with glue or tape. I gave the room a quick once over, hoping that nothing else had been destroyed, as I mentally calculated the cost to replace everything.

Let me set the scene. First, cue the darkest, scariest music you've ever heard, and that's the soundtrack to this part of the story. My glance rested on my computer screen, and I saw the most ominous words ever.

"Beware, your device will disengage momentarily due to unstable connections." Seconds later, my computer popped and immediately died a quick death. Hobie sat in the middle of this chaos with the frayed cables in his mouth. His innocent expression seemed to be asking me who had made this awful mess.

Weeks passed and Hobie's anxious behavior escalated. Every time I left the house, even for a small errand, Hobie demolished something. The vet explained that separation anxiety was pretty typical in dogs, even those who weren't rescues. Separation anxiety is triggered when dogs become upset because of being separated from the people they're attached to.

As I absorbed this information and wondered if I could afford to keep Hobie, the vet showed me a picture of the interior of a house that was a total wreck and then asked me if my house resembled that. As I nodded, I realized that a picture was worth more than a thousand words.

I left the office feeling exhausted and discouraged. My busy life was not what Hobie needed. Getting another dog to keep Hobie company was not a good option, and I refused to sedate him while I was gone. I did the only thing I knew to do. I put this problem in God's hands to solve. Then, I watched and waited for an answer.

I had to go out of town a short time later and needed to make arrangements for his care while I was gone. A neighbor offered to dogsit while I was out of town. When she and her three children came to pick up Hobie, I saw his demeanor change. The minute he saw them, his eyes brightened, and he leaped into the car with the kids. He seemed to smile from ear to ear as he licked each new face.

I had told her about the damage he had done to my home and belongings, thanks to separation anxiety. She assured me that Hobie would not be left alone. She had three busy children, one stay-at-home dad, a lab named Sam, and a cage of roosters in the back yard.

As I stood in the driveway, I knew the answer to my doggie dilemma. I loved Hobie, but he needed so many things that I couldn't give him. I was single and had a busy life. He needed a home with a big family, several kids, and lots of attention. I knew Hobie's best life couldn't be with me. I needed to muster the courage to give my dog away. And how would I ever do that?

After some rather long and sleepless nights, I realized my time with Hobie had been a rare blessing. Unknowingly, I was his brief step to something much better. I was Hobie's advocate, and this time it was all about his needs, not mine.

That family of five welcomed Hobie into their happy clan with open arms. They were all delighted to be together. As I walked away, I was both sad and uncertain as to whether I'd done the right thing. I would miss my new buddy. Despite his antics, Hobie had stolen my heart.

Weeks later, I visited Hobie's new home just to check on him. Sitting on their back porch, I watched him play fetch with his four-legged brother, Sam. As his new mama called him to come, that dog who had stolen my heart made a complete beeline to her. Watching him race to his mama, I noticed Hobie didn't run in circles. He galloped to her in an almost perfectly straight line.

At that moment, everything just clicked. I realized that Hobie's anxiety was gone and happiness filled its space. Although it was a tough call, I had made the right decision to give my bouncy boy away. Hobie was happy, healthy, and thriving in his new world.

As I made my way home, I felt proud to be Hobie's half-way house. It just goes to show you that sometimes you can't hold tightly to love when it needs to be given away.

CHAPTER SEVEN

NEW ENGLAND ASTERS
PATIENCE

UNWAVERING LOVE

*"In almost every garden, the land is made better
and so is the gardener."*
— Robert Rodale

I came into this whole gardening thing kicking and screaming. I moved to Wisconsin from Hawaii, the land of flamboyant and wildly amazing tropical flowers. We arrived in March, and by May, we saw that we had inherited a back yard of weeds, a garage that had seen better days, and mud where a path would later become a walkway to the back porch.

That same year, we got a dog. Not only was I one of those I'll-never-garden people, but I stood firmly in the I'll-never-get-a-dog camp. I was pretty committed to doing neither. For the record, I was also never going to move from Hawaii to the mainland. And yet, against my better judgment, here we are.

Last year we gardened in a drought. The first time I ever gardened was when I was in the Peace Corps in Mali, West Africa. I had a vegetable garden, and we made a tent of mosquito netting to keep out the birds and insects and whatever else wanted to feast on the veggies. I had to collect water once a day at 4:30 in the morning, and if we overslept, well, there was always tomorrow. Of course add up enough tomorrows, and everything will be dead.

Every morning I'd hand-water my garden while sweating under that netting. Tomatoes, green peppers, and green beans. And cantaloupe. The biggest, juiciest, and sweetest melons I'd ever tasted.

With the lack of rain in Wisconsin, I kept remembering my African gardening experience. I reminded myself that everything we grow is ornamental and to provide a habitat for the bees and butterflies. We weren't trying to survive off of our efforts, but it was still a lot of work and the constant watering meant a much larger water bill. And yet this was the year I had agreed to be one of the six homes on the Oshkosh Garden Walk.

On the Saturday before the big day, we got to visit the other gardens as a group. Holy cow, there are some serious gardeners with some stunning and very creative yards. Every garden was different—you could see the work and the commitment, and everyone was worried about this beastly hot and almost-rainless year.

The Garden Club said we'd have between 300 to 400 people through our gardens that day. Their numbers were off, and we had 600 or more. I was worried about my dog, but he was an absolute champ. Gary sat on the porch with him and answered about a million questions. Coconut got a huge bone, lots of hugs and belly rubs, and only barked when I put him inside, and he realized the party was still happening. And so he came out and resumed making everyone's day.

We received as many questions about our 1875 house as we did about the garden. People loved learning about the terrace in front of the street, planted in native plants and grasses instead of the weedy sod we replaced. And they loved learning about the rain garden, even though not much was in bloom there.

All of those gardening aficionados weren't there three weeks later to witness the rambunctious flowers in every color of the rainbow. The thing about gardens is that not everything blooms at the same time. The owner of the nursery we'd worked with had laid out a plan that had plants blooming from June through October. Just when one plant was spent, another would burst forth, so we always had something to enjoy.

The last to bloom in our garden are the New England asters which symbolize love and patience. I had never seen an aster before and I guess I was expecting larger blooms that would be a brilliant burst of color at the end of the growing season. That is not what happened.

New England asters are tall and it takes a while for the blossom to appear. In fact, that first year, I thought they were weeds they were so common and dreary. When I was almost ready to call the nursery and ask for a refund a miracle happened. Overnight tiny blue and pink blooms appeared transforming that section of the yard.

New England asters remind me of my little rescue dog; he was easy to love but, in the beginning, I needed a ton of patience. When we went to the rescue, we saw dogs who were much more visually appealing than one who chose me. Coconut was skinny, he had kennel cough, and he was just a plain, brown dog.

Coconut was not the perfect dog, and I had my shortcomings as well. The first weekend we spent hundreds of dollars at the emergency vet after he fell down the stairs and could not stand or walk. We had to replace the custom silk drapes he destroyed that first night, he trashed my only pair of prescription glasses, and he chewed a hole out of two kitchen mats.

One of the discussion points that often comes up when a person is adopting a dog is whether to bring home a puppy or an adult. Ultimately, the answer depends on a person's circumstances and preferences. Regardless of the age or the breed, it takes time and patience for both humans and dogs to experience that unwavering love.

The aster isn't flashy, and some might find it easy to write them off as pedestrian and not worth the effort. But they are wrong. Last year we had a bumper crop of those blue and pink flowers, and every day they were swarmed by fat-bottomed bees and colorful butterflies.

The perfect relationship between a dog and his or her owner isn't an overnight thing. But with love and patience magic happens just as it does every October when the asters flower.

BABY HALLE'S LEGACY
Janet Pfeiffer

*"Never be embarrassed by how much you care
about animals and how they're treated."*
— Stephanie Feldstein

I frequently visit our local animal shelter. Sometimes I simply drop off of items they might need, and other times, like an October day in 2022, I might take time to meet some of the dogs.

I was not looking to add another four-legged companion to my home, but something told me to go back and visit. And that's when I saw her.

If fear had a picture, it would look like her. Skinny. Black and tan matted fur. Huddled in the back of her cage. I bent and gently called to her.

As she approached, her body language indicated that she had been severely abused. I put my hand near the bars of the cage. As she licked my finger, she wrapped her paw around my arm, tugging with every ounce of strength she could muster. Her wretched cry pleaded for me to save her. I knew in that instant that she was mine.

From the moment the shelter released her to me for adoption, Baby Halle and I had an unbreakable bond. It wasn't easy driving home with a forty-pound canine sitting in my lap, wedged between the steering wheel and my chest, arms wrapped tightly around my neck. Yet somehow, we made it home safely.

For the first seven years of her life, Baby Halle had never seen daylight. Leaves falling from trees terrified her. Loud noises sent her seeking refuge in safe places. Her footpads were as pink as a newborn puppy's. Her paws bled on her first walk on the rough pavement outside.

Her coat was dull and brittle; her skin marked with raw and bleeding hot spots.

Seven years of horrific living conditions led to a compromised immune system and a lifetime of anxiety. Her severe and chronic eye problems were moderately relieved with the application of daily medication and soothing eye baths. An oral exam revealed Halle's front teeth were tiny brown stubbles, gnawed down to the gum line from years of desperately trying to free herself from her steel prison.

Baby Halle was a victim of medical research. For seven years this precious little soul suffered, isolated in a barren laboratory cage. Like millions of other animals, she had been subjected to unspeakable experiments conducted on her under the guise of science. Her only human contacts were lab technicians who performed these tests on her. She suffered extensive mental, emotional, and physical damage as a result of her long, unforgiving ordeal behind closed doors.

Baby Halle and I enjoyed a remarkable life together for the next eight and a half years. We were inseparable. We walked for miles every morning and hiked in the mountains on the weekends. When my husband and I were building a house for my daughter, she accompanied us to the construction site. Although she gradually accepted one of our other dogs, she never learned to fully trust humans. Oddly enough, she never displayed any signs of aggression toward anyone.

Halle was never far from my side. As I sat typing in my home office, she'd search for me every ten minutes or so. I would promptly stop working, join her on the floor, hold her in my lap, and stroke her, whispering words of reassurance in her ears. She'd emit a soft groan letting me know she felt safe and loved. This was the only time she was ever truly relaxed. Eventually, she'd rejoin the other dogs in the family room, only to come back to me several minutes later.

Baby Halle made remarkable progress. I researched gemstones for healing and aromatherapy and supplements for calming and grounding her. She often disconnected mentally from her surroundings, a survival technique she had acquired during her time in isolation. Hematite helped to keep her grounded. Blue lace agate reduced anxiety. Lavender oil and valerian root added to her sense of calm. Lots of physical contact, petting, and massage also helped her sense of well-being.

Yet despite all my attempts to compensate for the years of horror she endured, she never fully recovered nor forgot her ordeal. On some level, she relived that nightmare every day. Baby Halle passed away suddenly on May 6, 2011 at the age of fifteen-and-a- half. The loss of every dog is unbearably painful, but I was totally unprepared for the magnitude of this one.

Bonding with a fur baby like Baby Halle comes along once in a lifetime and the pawprints these fur babies leave on our heart are profound and eternal. Although we adopted another dog two weeks later, and five more since, there will never be another quite like my precious little girl who sat in my lap hugging my neck as we drove the twenty-two miles from the shelter to her forever home.

I will always advocate against testing on animals. But because of this experience, I now only adopt senior dogs, severe abuse cases, or those with tragic histories. For like my Baby Halle, they are the most loving, forgiving, and loyal little souls on earth. This will forever be the legacy of my sweet Baby Halle.

DOING THE IMPOSSIBLE

*"Start by doing what's necessary; then do what's possible;
and suddenly you're doing the impossible."*
— Francis of Assisi

When Jim announced that we were closing the rescue two years after the start of COVID–19, the rush was on to find every dog a home. I was interviewed for stories in the local newspaper and on various television stations. Each reporter asked what would happen to the dogs that didn't find a family. I assured them that thirty days was more than enough time to get the word out, and we didn't anticipate any problems.

We'd worked with the high-kill shelter in Kentucky for ten years, and it was a devastating blow to them that we could no longer be there for the dogs who needed homes up north. Jim, the rescuer with a heart of gold, probably agreed to bring more canines on that last trip than he should have, but how could he say no?

The transport was filled with dogs much larger that the twenty-five-pound weight limit that many landlords set on pets. Certain breeds can be harder to place, and on that last transport there were many of those who needed a home.

We had two adoption events before closing and both vendor partners were fantastic about getting the word out and helping us in every way possible. The first Saturday we found homes for nine dogs! People also drove from all over Wisconsin to say thank you for all we had done. Many brought the dogs they had adopted from us and, while it was lovely to hear their stories and see the dogs that we had helped to find a home, it was a bittersweet day.

A few more dogs found homes before our final event which left us with six that needed to be adopted. Just when I was starting to feel like we could actually pull off the impossible, we got word from a group asking if we could help a mom and her puppies. They were out of state and would be euthanized if no one stepped up. We didn't have the resources and the clock was ticking. The puppies had been weaned and, the day before the scheduled date with death, mom had gotten adopted, so we said yes to the five homeless pups.

The weather was perfect for that last event; we saw lots of foot traffic and the puppies were a big hit. A number of faithful volunteers walked the larger dogs, adoption counselors expedited applications, and a few more dogs found their humans.

Everyone gravitated to one dog named Dottie. She was at that stage where she had outgrown the energy that can sometimes make cattle dogs and other herding breeds harder to place. Her luxurious black coat was turning gray and the splotches of dirty white fur here and there made her a one-of-a-kind girl. She was an over-seventy-five-pound senior, so it would take the right person to adopt her. But we knew it would happen.

People gave Dottie lots of love and hugs and kisses. We heard every reason why they couldn't adopt such a perfect dog: They were at their three-dog limit, they weren't allowed to get a dog that large; their partner said no way. One person made a donation to reduce Dottie's adoption fee. Then another person chipped in a bit. But no one seemed to be able to give her the good home she deserved.

As a couple of the puppies found takers and applications were completed for some of the adult dogs, I began to worry about Dottie. Jim lived on a farm and could take her, but I sensed someone special out there needed Dottie as much as she need him or her.

"Do you foster dogs?"

The red-headed woman seemed tentative, almost like she knew she wasn't going to get the answer she wanted.

"No, I'm sorry; we don't have a foster program," I explained. "All of our dogs go straight from our building to their forever homes."

Her shoulders slumped, and she looked like she'd been turned down before. Her friend whispered something, and they began to walk away.

At that moment I knew; Dottie was the perfect dog for them. I caught up with the dejected women and asked if one of them had an approved application. The first woman explained that she had not completed an application with us, but she had applied and been turned down everywhere she tried, which was why she had asked about fostering. She suffered from anxiety, which some people thought meant she could not take care of a dog. As she explained how important it was for her to have an emotional support animal, I felt a connection.

I found one of the counselors and asked if she could work with a potential adopter. I explained that the woman needed a calm dog, that a puppy would probably not work.

The counselor went over the application asking for clarification on some questions. One reason for being denied was that she didn't have landlord approval, and that is a requirement for every rescue or shelter. The last thing we wanted was for the dog to be returned when the landlord realized a dog was living there.

They had just moved into their new place. It had lots of room and a fenced yard, and she thought it would be okay. She called the property owner and explained that she had found a large dog to adopt. After a few responses to the person on the phone, she asked the counselor for our email. Within a short time the landlord sent his permission for them to adopt a dog with no size limitation.

Bright and early the next day, we sent Dottie home with a leash and a collar, a few toys, and a huge bag of dog food to get them started. She was the last adult dog and, because of the money others gave to help this one special pooch, her fee ended up being only $50.00.

A few months later I walked into a small pet store in town, and I saw a one-of-a-kind dog with a black coat that was turning gray with splotches of dirty white fur here and there. Her owners were laughing and talking and excited, as they discussed what toys and treats to buy for their girl.

Dottie is now Honey, and you'll never meet a happier, more beautifully trained girl.

Her owners both gave me hugs and thanked me for helping when no one else would.

Finding homes for Dottie and all of the other dogs in our care seemed an impossible task. But at the last event of a ten-year dream, the impossible happened.

I felt like Walt Disney when he said, "It's kind of fun to do the impossible."

MOLLY'S MARVELOUS FAMILY
Carolyn Fisher

"A small pet is often an excellent companion."
— Florence Nightingale

After losing Kelsey, our cavalier king Charles spaniel we had only had shy of three years, my husband and I both decided we would not get another dog. The heartbreak of her abrupt departure was terrible. We gave away everything except her picture and settled into being just the two of us. A year later, in 2015, my husband died of brain cancer.

If you have ever been attached to an animal, you know the companionship and unconditional love it brings you. After my losses so close together, the memories in the empty house were too much, and before long, I asked my daughter if she could help me find another puppy.

She was in the dog business and knew many reputable breeders. I knew she would find the perfect pet/companion for me. Sure enough, when I got off a flight from visiting my other daughter, her sister picked me up with the promised pup.

The adorable little puppy, who looked like a bear cub, was the runt of the litter, and the owners were getting rid of it. I asked what kind it was, and she said it was a shih-poo which is a shih tzu mixed with a toy poodle. I named her Molly; it just seemed to fit. Soon after, when I took her to the groomer, he suggested a puppy cut, and we never changed because it was cute and suited her.

Molly and I bonded quickly. She needed me as much as I needed her. Molly was smart, and she was the love of my life. I felt happier and more carefree than I had in quite some time.

I told Molly every day how much I loved her and how special she was to me. I would sit in my easy chair and call her to sit in my lap, tickling her ears and rubbing her tummy. The love we had for each other was immeasurable.

The wonderful thing about puppies is that they exude happiness and are always up for fun. She quickly learned that when I said, "Let's play ball," that was the cue for her to run to get a toy from her box. She would choose from the wide selection of playthings I spoiled her with—a tug rope, a squeaky bone, and even a ball that I filled with peanut butter. That was one of her favorite treats.

We took short walks during the day and cuddled together every night. But all too soon, age and health challenges meant that I needed to move into an independent living community. Unfortunately, it didn't allow dogs.

I had grown so attached to Molly that it broke my heart, but the family who took her were friends of my younger daughter, and they had two other dogs.

I often wish dogs could share how they feel beyond body language and their expressive eyes. Molly must have wondered why I took her crate and an empty box and placed them by the front door. I slowly began putting all of Molly's stuff in the box, one thing at a time. When I picked up her bowls from the floor and took her food from the pantry, Molly began to tremble. I looked into her intelligent eyes and saw fear, something I had never seen before. She was such an intuitive little thing and seemed to know something had changed.

Soon, all of Molly's belongings were waiting at the door. I leaned over, picked her up, and hugged her tightly. We sat in our chair where we cuddled and watched television. Then, a big wet teardrop fell from my eyes and slid down Molly's nose. She whimpered, thinking she had done something to make me so sad.

I sighed when I realized that it was time for her new family to arrive.

When a dog or a spouse dies, there are no words to express the loss. I truly had no idea that, in some ways, sending my devoted companion to live with another family would be, in its own way, just as horrible.

The doorbell rang, and I scooted Molly off my lap and went to answer the door. The woman bent to pat Molly on the head, but Molly darted behind me. Molly didn't do her happy dance at the door. Instead, she sat quietly as we loaded her belongings into the waiting car.

When everything was gone, I picked up Molly, carried her outside to the car, and placed a heart-shaped pillow in her crate. "Molly," I said barely able to hide my tears, "I hope this pillow I made for you reminds you of how much you are loved, and how special you will always be to me. Be brave. I will come to see you soon."

I noticed two other crates in the back seat. One of them held an older dog who I later learned was Gracie. She didn't seem happy about the newest member of the family. Sophie Sue, the younger dog, seemed ready for a new playmate and wagged her tail excitedly.

Molly's new home included a fenced yard with room to frolic by herself, with her new sisters, or with her new humans. Their house was huge compared my house.

Molly was used to living with one quiet person, and now she had two dogs and two humans. I hoped she would see all these changes as good and that she would soon feel like she was exactly where she belonged.

I missed her terribly, but the family offered to let me visit my precious Molly. A week later, I was invited to Molly's gotcha party. As soon as she spotted me, Molly frolicked over. I scooped her into my arms. I held her tight and whispered to her how much I loved her and how special she was.

We all went outside, and it was a joy to see Molly playing with her two doggy sisters and the bulldog from next door. I knew that, as hard as it was for me, it was the perfect choice for Molly. Before leaving, I picked her up for another squeeze and reassured her that I would be back to visit as soon as I could. Molly gave me a slobbery kiss in return.

Molly now has a big, marvelous, adopted family who recognize that her first mama will always have a special place in her heart, even though she doesn't live with her. She now has two sisters, two mamas, a papa, and two doggy friends.

Molly's marvelous family truly makes her feel special and loved. They bring her to see me, which thrills my heart. And she remembers me, and she knows she will always have a place in my heart.

I am glad I chose to adopt that teddy bear of a puppy with a heart big enough to love her new family and me. Molly is the last dog I will ever adopt. She is also the best. And even though she doesn't live with me any longer, she continues to be a huge help as I navigate these changes in my life.

Molly never dreamed that being rescued would have given her so much. Neither did I. Neither of us could have asked for anything better.

MIKO AND ME
by Charles Dakin as told to Zeta Davidson

*"For a man living alone, dogs are almost
more important than human beings."*
— Richard Katz

A year after I lost my wife of fifty years, I had a routine down. The days blended into each other, and the overwhelming quiet made me question why I even got up each day.

Others had lost their longtime partners to death, and they had found different ways of coping. One wrote about her grief, another moved to a senior housing community. I'm not a writer, and I was fully capable of taking care of myself. Besides, the house was paid for. So there I stayed, wondering how to fill the emptiness now that I was alone.

My late wife was a quilter, and she'd spent hours at her quilting machine, creating works of art. I'd watch television or find other ways to fiddle around. We weren't attached at the hip at all times, but, somehow, having her there even when we didn't talk to each other was comforting.

I'm not sure why I did a search online after checking my email that day. Probably because I wasn't ready to leave my office and head back downstairs to the quiet. Instead, I typed in Kansas City Pet Project—the name of a no-kill animal shelter near me.

I'm not the kind to sit with a small, fuzzy dog in my lap all afternoon, so my search went to larger-sized pups. I searched for older, house-trained dogs that would not want to eat leather shoes or chew on my recliner. I probably looked for a month, and I even expanded my search to include a rescue group called Wayside Waifs and the Kansas City SPCA.

Two possibilities caught my eye, so I drove to KC Pet Project to see which one I liked best. My first choice paid zero attention to me. And then I met Miko. He really chose me.

He did have some things going on—he was three-legged, had a bad case of heartworm, and had been brought back twice before.

The shelter identified restraint issues. I was told he may have been abused. Miko had come to the shelter as a stray puppy, had been adopted and brought back, adopted again for three years only to be returned. I was delighted when Miko, who was mostly German shepherd, came running toward me.

Interestingly, he has not misbehaved with me. He had already started his four months of heartworm treatment, so I took him back again and again. Adopting from a shelter has many benefits and, in Miko's case, the heartworm treatments were covered from start to finish. If I'd taken him to the local veterinarian, that would have been $1700.00 out of my pocket.

Miko is very smart and trainable. He likes to play and does well on a leash. I do not turn him loose because if neighbors were to see an eighty-pound dog running toward them, they would probably be scared to death. He does enjoy chasing squirrels, but will turn to see if I am near.

At the shelter's recommendation I hired a trainer, and we worked together for three months. Miko learned leash behavior and not getting so distracted and pulling on our daily walks. He is still reactive when visitors come to the door, but as soon as I say, "Place," he doesn't charge the door. Because he has only three legs, he does not have a leash strolling speed. He lopes—thus moves faster than a normal dog.

He enjoys a few people foods; I just do an online search to see if what he wants is okay for him to have. So far, he enjoys frozen blueberries, Greek yogurt, and an occasional scrambled egg. To add some much-needed weight to his frame, some days I make him a puppuccino. I call them pup cups, and our version is steamed oat milk foamed like a latte.

I haven't had to set an alarm since I've had him. He stands by my bed in the morning until I get up to take him out. I don't have to worry about him jumping on the couch—impossible without his other leg. I also try to not make him go upstairs from my office to the rest of the house—we walk outside around the house and go in the sliding glass door, so he doesn't have strain on his one back leg. You might think, like other dogs, he would watch television with me—nope, not interested. He'd rather snooze.

Probably because of losing his leg and all of the heartworm treatments, Miko hates going to the vet. I can't say I blame him. We've made several social visits at the request of his trainer and the veterinarian—we go, get out of my truck, and go into the office each week for five minutes and then leave. You'd think week after week of doing this would help. It didn't. Miko still needs sedation when his name is called to be seen.

I'm seventy-seven and Miko is seven, which makes him a senior like me. I've gotten more attached than I ever thought I would to a dog—and a handicapped rescue dog at that.

Miko isn't a noisy dog and, for the most part, the house is still quiet. But we're inseparable and somehow his very presence is enough to give me a reason to make it seventy-eight or however many years I'm given.

Instead of burrowing under the covers and wondering why I should get out of bed, thanks to Miko, I have a reason to enjoy life.

"Come on, Miko," I tell my best friend each day. "Let's go to my truck to see what adventure we can find today."

COCONUT FARTS

*"You can say any foolish thing to a dog, and the dog
will give you a look that says, 'Wow, you're right!
I never would've thought of that!'*
— Dave Barry

One day a few years ago we met a little girl on our neighborhood walk. She was about three at the time, I was surprised that she was without a parent or an older sibling.

She rushed to us, hand outstretched, and I told Coconut to sit. She was going to pet that dog no matter what I did or said, and she knelt down with her hand almost touching his snout. Coconut is friendly, and he's used to people approaching him, but the last thing we needed was for her to startle my dog and get nipped or worse.

"Don't touch his face," I instructed as I guided her little hand to the middle of my pup's back. "You never want to scare a dog."

As she rubbed his fur back and forth and up and down, I again wondered why she was alone. She didn't seem neglected, and she started singing some sort of tune so quietly I could barely hear. She turned her precious face to peer at me and smiled.

"What's his name?"

"His name is Coconut," I answered.

Her nose wrinkled and she hesitated just a bit and then asked me a question. "Why does he smell like coconut?"

It took a couple of beats for me to remember I had put coconut oil on my hands and legs before leaving the house. I explained this to her, and she grinned.

"Oh, I thought he had coconut farts!"

She laughed so hard she fell to the ground. Coconut decided it was play time, and they rolled around on the grass next to the sidewalk. She squealed, he barked, and I laughed at such a perfect picture of unleashed joy.

After a few minutes of rambunctious play she ran inside to tell her mom about coconut farts. The family moved away a year or so later, but before that, whenever we'd pass her house she'd see us, run outside, place her hand on Coconut's back, and rub his fur back and forth and up and down.

Every few days during the dry winter I use coconut oil on my arms, legs and feet. Coconut knows where I store it. When I open the drawer and take out the jar, he seems to think he is getting an extra treat.

I made sure that coconut oil was safe for him to eat, and the vet said no more than one teaspoonful, which is significantly more than he has ever had at one time.

A dog will make you laugh and give you more joy than you ever thought possible. And, so far, I guess coconut agrees with him because I've yet to smell coconut farts.

THE CHANGING OF THE GUARD
Anne Foley Rauth

"Because of the dog's joyfulness, our own is increased.
It is no small gift."
— Mary Oliver

Our rescue dog, Abbie the Labbie, was the queen of the household and acted as if the world revolved around her. In all honesty, she wasn't wrong. Things were done in a certain way, schedules kept, and Abbie was quite content with the status quo never changing. Until it did.

One snowy January day, instead of four muddy paw prints on our hardwood floor, there were eight. Those four extra prints came courtesy of a puppy that was more change than twelve-year-old Abbie wanted. She was ready to live out her retirement days kicking back and napping, not having her world turned upside down.

When I learned that some puppies needed foster families I had decided to help out. On the plus side, our oldest son, a college graduate back living with us, agreed to help me foster one of the puppies. The other reason I said yes to being a foster grandparent to Holly the Collie is that I figured it would be a short-term title. Everyone knew that puppies get adopted quickly so we wouldn't have time to bond and, for Abbie, it would be a minor inconvenience.

We expected that Holly would be adorable. She was a puppy and a collie, so that was kind of a given. But we didn't expect that she would be petrified of both humans and dogs. Instead of getting to know her surroundings and playing with Abbie, the scared puppy buried her head in our oldest son's lap and would not come out. Her cute little whimpers made everyone come to see what was wrong.

Abbie did not appreciate being toppled from her queenly throne. She could not understand who this new dog was and why it was in her castle, stealing the attention from her. She went from barely tolerating this little usurper to being downright rude, barking and nipping at Holly whenever she came near her.

Holly soon decided this was her home and that the old girl wouldn't stop her from fitting in where she belonged. Holly had come from a family of several siblings and couldn't understand why this dog overlord did not want to play with her nonstop.

Holly quickly caught on to the routines of our household. All three of our sons loved her. She would play, wrestle and fetch—three things Abbie had grown tired of doing. Deep down, Abbie was holding on to the hope that the word *foster* meant *short term*.

Holly ended up being a foster fail when our oldest son adopted her. Abbie finally realized that the foster meant forever, and she became a mother figure to the puppy. She taught her how to go outside, encouraged her to chase squirrels in our backyard, and showed her where—and where not—to nap.

At times, Abbie inwardly shook her head in disgust at this new dog in the house, especially when Holly was close to Abbie's food or a favorite napping spot. But gradually, Abbie has come around and seems to miss Holly when she goes on adventures with our son.

Now a year after Holly's gotcha day, roles have reversed. Abbie is suffering from congestive heart failure and coughs quite a bit. She cannot go up the stairs in our house anymore. Holly now takes care of her. Whenever she hears Abbie coughing, Holly races to her side, even if Abbie is several floors away.

Abbie still loves to go on neighborhood walks, but she can't go as far or as fast as her protégé-turned-caregiver. Our family got an all-terrain cart that we call "the carriage" for Queen Abbie to ride in. One day, while out walking, our oldest son got tired of pulling the Queen, so he tied Holly's leash to the handle, and Holly started pulling her friend. The caravan is quite a sight to see when we are out walking.

When they both go out in our backyard for some recreation and relaxation, Abbie cannot chase the squirrels anymore and will only bark at them. Holly may not bark, but she is fast and can chase them away, and the team effort does the trick.

Recently in the middle of the night, my husband and I awoke to a ferocious ruckus—Holly was barking, and our first thought, given the severity of the barking, was that intruders had come in our home. When we arrived downstairs, we realized that once again, Holly was taking care of her friend, Abbie. Somehow Abbie's tail had knocked the bathroom door shut. Abbie was being held captive in a tiny room and needed to be released from the small room.

This team effort is a philosophy I wish more humans would adapt. Instead of being combative with one another, why not divide and conquer and use each of our strengths to compliment others and to help society in general?

We don't know how much longer Abbie will be with us, but we will cherish every day we have with her, as will Holly, her old nemesis. Dogs teach us so much. Abbie and Holly teach a great lesson that understanding that whatever our challenges—whether they be squirrels in the yard, or a work situation that will take more than one department to solve—celebrating both youth and seniors is a win-win.

TEDDY KNEW
Mary J. Hahn

"A dog has one aim in life . . . to bestow his heart."
— Writer and editor J.R. Ackerley

I never grew up with dogs—maybe because in a house with nine active children, we had no room or time for them. I didn't dislike the idea of being a pet owner, but, as a single mom, I followed my parents' decision to be a no-dog home.

My youngest daughter came at me with every argument every kid has when he or she wants a dog. Margaret would feed him. She'd make sure he didn't make a mess, of course she'd walk him, and whatever dog she got would not be my problem.

The summer before she started sixth grade, a fluffy, white, and completely adorable puppy adopted us. His full name was Teddy Polar Bear, but we called him Teddy, Theodore, Bear, Teddy Bear, Bear Boy, and probably a few other names. I still wasn't convinced I wanted this lifestyle change, but, little by little, Teddy wormed his way into my heart.

Unlike most dogs I knew, Teddy stayed in that cute puppy mode his entire life.

Mom had given birth to her children in the 1940s, '50s, '60s, and '70s. If anyone needed a rest from taking care of living breathing beings, it was her. You would think she would want to finally be free of diapers and the terrible-two tantrums. But she embraced my daughters, and they embraced her back.

I worked full time, and Mom helping with the girls through the various stages of their lives, allowed me to have a career. When Teddy came into our lives, she embraced him, as well. Eventually, as the girls grew to need less hands-on care before and after school, her focus turned to Teddy, and she became his.

We lived only four blocks from my parents' home. Each morning, Mom would walk over to collect Teddy, spend the day with him, and then she'd walk him back before the girls got home from their after-school activities. She wanted him there to "protect the girls."

As kids do, Josephine and Margaret grew up and went to college. And as grandmas do, Mom got older and frailer and unable to safely walk a still-boisterous dog. Teddy visited her during weekend walks with me when I was off work. During the week, my nephew-turned-dogwalker faithfully made sure that Ted got to my mom's every day.

Time passed, and after many, many walks and visits, my mom got older and even frailer. First, she had a stroke. Then she was diagnosed with Guillain-Barre, a rare disorder in which your body's immune system attacks your nerves. She fully recovered from the stroke, but Guillain-Barre' had her on life support in less than a week, and she just wasn't able to fully physically recover.

Teddy visited her while she was in the nursing home getting strong enough to come home. She reached down to pet him from her bed, and oh man, both were in heaven. Teddy got older too, and found it more and more difficult to walk the four blocks to my parents' home. Those walks got harder and shorter until he just couldn't visit my mom on his own. We used a ramp to get him into our car so we could drive him over to see her.

Our family has pulled through many challenges. We kept hoping and praying that mom would get better and that the quality of her life would improve. We had no way of knowing it was her last year. Not enough adjectives exist to describe how incredibly tough of a year it was on Mom, but also on us all.

It was like playing Whac A Mole, when one symptom led to a diagnoses only to be followed by something new and equally awful. Each time the doctors, my dad, and Mom handled one medical emergency, another one popped up. But she always made it through.

Then, one Friday while I was at work, I got a call from an unrecognized number that I let go to voice mail. I didn't check the message until I was stuck in bumper-to-bumper traffic on my way home. I hit the button to play the message. My brother had called from his new cell phone to let me know that Mom was dying.

I inched my way along, wishing I could make all of the cars move so I could get home and see my mom. By the time I got to the house, she was already gone. My dad sat across from his wife of sixty-three years looking with disbelief at her lifeless body. And there, at her feet, was Teddy.

My nephew, the dog walker, didn't have a car. No one else knew how Teddy, the dog with such an amazing bond with my mom, had gotten to the house.

All we can figure out is that Teddy knew. He knew that the woman who never wanted a dog, the one who opened her home and her heart to him, had struggled to walk over one last time.

Teddy and my mom had twelve special years together. The bond between the dog and woman was so strong that Teddy knew. Nothing was going to keep him away from saying goodbye to his friend. We will never know how Teddy knew. But we do believe that Mom sensed his presence in that room. I wish I would have had one last time to hold her hand and say goodbye. Teddy took my place that day, as both he and my mom had done countless times with my girls.

I will always miss my mom and Teddy. And I will always be grateful for their special friendship, and that, on the day when it mattered the most, Teddy knew.

CHAPTER EIGHT

PHLOX
COMPATIBILITY

MY MOST COMPATIBLE COMPANION

*"Old age means realizing you will never own
all the dogs you wanted to."*
— Joe Gores

In 2020, my husband was out for the entire gardening season with prostate cancer surgery and a hip replacement. He's cancer-free now, but that was not my favorite summer of gardening.

My next-door neighbor passed away that same year. Rich had been a master gardener and had a lovely yard. Knowing how quickly weeds can take over, I decided to see if he had anything I could rescue. I'm glad I had taken some black-eyed Susans while he was still alive and that he had already given me a cutting from his favorite bleeding heart plant. When they both explode into gorgeous color each spring and fall, I remember his kindness and gardening talent.

I strolled throughout his yard with my phone and several apps trying to differentiate between a weed and a viable plant. Some beautiful weeds masquerade as flowers. The last thing I wanted was to transplant the wrong thing and have it overtake the other plants. I had paid good money for those plants.

I focused on the leaves, since most of what was in the ground had yet to bloom. The verdict from the various apps all pointed to a phlox. They were so overgrown that I thought it was one giant bush and not individual plants.

Not only did I not have Gary to help me, but before we could move the phlox, the entire east side of the house had to be cleared of the dreaded orange ditch lilies, an invasive flower that can spread both by spreading rhizomes, and by long trailing roots spreading from their clumps.

These flowers can crowd out other native perennials and they are also not particularly attractive to pollinators.

This was an exceptionally hot summer and the task involved back-breaking labor. I have never been prouder of creating something as I was of rescuing those fuchsia phlox. And Coconut was with me every step of the way.

Because the area isn't fenced and we live on a busy street, I put a stake and a six-foot lead into the ground where I worked. As I dug out those lilies and cursed more than a little, Coconut watched for squirrels and, when they didn't appear, he snoozed. When I'd move to another section, I'd relocate his lead so he'd never be far away.

I was such a newbie that I asked members of the Wisconsin Gardening Facebook group questions every step of the way. The good news is that every plant made it! I've learned that, like dog owners, gardeners are generous. When I asked what to plant in front of the phlox, several people in that group offered me some sedum. I drove to different cities picking up these rescue plants that now stand in front of the cream city brick of our home.

I love the east side of the house because it's all rescue plants, and I accomplished everything by myself. And I never want to do it again. I had just turned sixty-five, which is a pretty late age to start major projects like this. I walk my dog during full bloom season, and every time I pass this side of the house, I stop and marvel at what I achieved with rescue plants and hard work.

Phlox symbolize harmony and compatibility, which is a perfect way to describe dogs. Coconut is my most compatible friend. He is happy doing anything from taking a long walk to a snooze on the end of the sofa while I read. He'll watch any television show, eat whatever I give him, and he knows when I need an extra dose of love after a bad day.

Rescue dogs have much to give, and something is special about what they bring to us as we move into this phase of our lives.

Being Coconut's mom for over six years I've learned that, like plants, dogs are resilient and they add more to our lives than I ever thought possible. There's a learning curve, no matter what new things we tackle in life, but, with gardening and dogs, it's worth every effort, every dollar, and every bit of time invested.

KARLIE'S LESSONS
Andie LaComb

"Dogs die. But dogs live, too. They live brave, beautiful lives.
They protect their families. And love us.
And make our lives a little brighter. And they don't
waste time being afraid of tomorrow."
— Dan Gemeinhart

A few months before we said goodbye to Jasmine, our sixteen-year-old border collie, we adopted eleven-month-old, Anna, another border collie. The two of them quickly bonded, but three months later, we said goodbye to Jasmine. Anna was completely lost without her. Even though she'd had such a brief time with her big sister, Anna seemed bereft at being the only canine in the house.

The obvious solution was to adopt another rescue to be Anna's friend. I soon found Karlie, a four-month-old Catahoula/Australian shepherd/ mix. I thought she might be too rambunctious for Anna, but decided to set up a meet and greet. Their time together was so successful that we brought Karlie home for a sleepover

That afternoon and evening were the happiest I had seen Anna since she had become an only pooch. The two girls wrestled, chased each other, and then fell asleep before starting all over again. We quickly decided Karlie would make a perfect addition to our family.

For nearly twelve years Anna and Karlie were best friends doing everything together. They loved running alongside the pool while I swam, followed by a rest on the lounge chairs in the backyard. Together we explored the park, and they were both great kayakers. True to her breed, Anna herded Karlie like she was her personal sheep. When Karlie chased tennis balls in the backyard, she played defense, making it more challenging for Karlie to bring the ball back to me. Anytime they were resting, some part of their bodies had to be touching.

Shortly after Anna's twelfth birthday, she started to have seizures. We managed her symptoms for several months until the medication no longer controlled them, and she had multiple seizures in a twenty-four-hour period. We decided it was time to say goodbye and made the dreaded appointment.

We celebrated her for a week, doing all her favorite things. On her last day, we took her to the park to run off leash, spent time in our back-yard, had ice cream and cake, and took one final walk to the vet. We gave Anna endless kisses and whispered sweet nothings in her ear. And then she was gone.

On the walk home, we missed our sweet Anna, and I started to think how lonely Karlie was going to be. That's when I decided Karlie and I needed to keep busy to help us not miss Anna so much.

Every week I searched the internet, looking for a new place to visit. We traveled all over San Diego, exploring beaches, canyons, and trails. A short time after an excursion where we climbed a literal mountain, I noticed Karlie starting to slow down, to pant more during walks in our neighborhood, and to gag and cough after drinking water.

We took her to the vet, but the only diagnosis was arthritis and the typical aging process. She continued to have issues and even started to lose her bark. That's when I googled her symptoms and stumbled upon Geriatric Onset Laryngeal Paralysis Polyneuropathy (GOLPP), a degenerative disease that impairs the esophagus, larynx, and hind legs. The cause is unknown and there is no cure. We took her to a surgeon who confirmed the diagnosis.

After months of trial and error, including some dietary changes and new medication, we were able to reduce the gagging/coughing, which was caused by acid reflux. We adapted to her changes in stamina by shortening our walks and going earlier in the day, when it was cooler. This allowed us to manage her hind end weakness and to continue to have adventures in San Diego and eventually Bloomington, Indiana, where we moved several months later.

After our move to Indiana, the disease continued to progress slowly, taking away Karlie's ability to walk. To help her we covered all the non-carpeted floors with packing blankets to improve her traction, put sneakers on her back paws, did indoor physical therapy to strengthen her back legs, and eventually purchased a rear-wheel wheelchair for her to use on her walks and adventures.

We started using the wheelchair in our basement in Indiana, doing laps until she was accustomed to it. Once she felt comfortable, we transitioned to our backyard and, eventually, went on walks in our neighborhood and on paved trails.

In the fall, we made the cross-country trip from Bloomington to San Diego for the winter. Karlie attracted a lot of attention as she wheeled into the hotel elevator and up to our room each night. When we arrived in San Diego, she quickly became the celebrity of our neighborhood with people stopping us on our walks to ask about her wheels. I was always happy to explain how well they worked and gave people information on where to purchase them.

She seemed to thrive and blossom the first three months we were back in San Diego. We visited with friends and returned to some of our favorite hiking places. We even purchased a stand-up paddle board and took her kayaking on Mission Bay. She was used to kayaking in our sit-on-top boat, but quickly learned how to sit on the front of the SUP board and be the captain.

We were all happy and having such a great time being back in San Diego. Karlie even strengthened the muscle in her back legs and no longer needed to use her wheelchair. People who had seen her using her wheels made comments about how well she was doing without them. I was so proud of her and happy to see her doing well.

And then, suddenly, she lost her appetite and eventually stopped eating altogether. She was nauseated and had episodes of vomiting and diarrhea. Despite a visit to the vet, the only diagnosis was anemia caused by a chronic condition. He prescribed meds, but on the second day of taking them, Karlie told us she was ready to go. When I took her out in the morning she struggled to walk and was disoriented. After peeing she stood and stared off into space. I knelt next to her and said "It's time, isn't it baby girl?"

She struggled to walk across the street, so I picked her up, carried her down the alley, hugging her and telling her it would be okay. Once I got her inside and settled on her bed, I spoke to my husband. We decided it was time, and I called and made the appointment for that afternoon.

Although we only had a few hours, we made the most of them and took her to the beach, one of her favorite places. The three of us sat on the sand enjoying every last minute together. After about an hour, we headed back to our condo, where we waited to take her to her last appointment. We gave her as much love and attention as we could.

Her last gift to us was her signature smile, just before she got her wings. We sent her off with kisses, hugs, and a lifetime of memories. We loved all our girls, but this goodbye was the hardest and most painful. I didn't know how I would manage without my hiking and adventure partner.

Nearly seven months passed before I came to terms with her being gone. Despite adopting another dog, I still miss Karlie and taking her on adventures. I learned many lessons from Karlie, the biggest one being that every day is an adventure and to make them all count.

NOT "JUST A DOG"
Roxanne Rolph

"Sorrow is how we learn to love. Your heart isn't breaking.
It hurts because it's getting larger.
The larger it gets, the more love it holds."
— Rita Mae Brown

Like many people, I was raised by parents who believed a dog was just a dog—an animal that was nothing more than a possession. A thing, if you will. At times, our dogs would be kept outside, they were not taken to the vet, and they certainly were not allowed to sleep on our beds or be treated in any other way like a family member. It wasn't just dogs; we had a cat that was never taken to the vet either.

Sadly, our family cat ended up getting leukemia, which was passed along to my mother when the cat scratched her. My parents weren't mean or uncaring; they were simply unknowing. And while that doesn't make their attitude right; it does explain it.

I was unhappy to see our dogs and cat treated like this. I knew it wasn't right, but I wouldn't have been able to get my parents to understand. Not only was I just a kid, I didn't understand, or even know, the true love of a dog. Family dogs weren't given a chance to fully demonstrate that kind of love. I wish I knew then what I know now, because I possibly could have conveyed to my parents the proper way to treat a dog or cat. If so, our pets might have had better lives.

When I was in my early thirties and married with two kids, my husband and I adopted our first dog, Brutus. Our handsome black Labrador was a family dog in every sense of the word. Maybe because

I wanted to make sure Brutus never lived the kind of life my child-hood pets had lived, we emphasized the word *family*.

We had the pleasure of loving, and being loved unconditionally by Brutus for ten glorious years. Sadly, he was diagnosed with bone cancer and, six weeks later, we had to have him put down. I was crushed. Our hearts ached. The kids also felt it. We experienced the grief on differ-ent levels, given the difference in our ages and that of our children. I spent nearly every day crying over the loss. My husband thought getting another dog might help, so two months later, we met, fell in love with, and adopted a beautiful six-week-old purebred chocolate Labrador we named Phoenix.

Even though I still missed Brutus considerably, having Phoenix gave me the chance to love another dog and, as with Brutus, give her uncondi-tional love. I believe that's what Brutus would have wanted. Somehow it almost seemed like Brutus sent Phoenix to us, to help us deal with our grief.

Last year, we had our hearts broken again when we lost eleven-year-old Phoenix to cancer. She'd been part of our family a little lon-ger than Brutus had, and because I was older and had learned over the years to love a pet even more deeply, I felt the passing of Phoenix even more profoundly.

Through our having Brutus and Phoenix as family pets, my father finally understood that pets were family members, not just animals that families kept. He still thought they were just dogs, but he also under-stood why we felt and shared the love with them that we did. And the love I experienced and shared with Phoenix even furthered my love for animals and gave me a greater outlook and understanding about how all animals need us—not just dogs or cats. So I now treat any animal I may encounter with a deeper understanding and greater level of care. I have Phoenix and Brutus to thank for that.

While my husband and I have not yet been able to bring ourselves to share our lives and love with another dog, I believe that someday we will. And I believe that Phoenix will help us find that next family dog—just as Brutus helped us find Phoenix.

THE PERFECT SLEEP AID

"The truth is that it's just really hard for me to get to sleep without a dog in my bedroom."
— Jimmy Stewart

"Grandma, some stores are open right now."

"No, Steven. Everything is closed. Now go to sleep."

My five-year-old grandson wasn't ready to drop the subject.

"Grandma, there are places still open. There's the gas station with the store inside. They never close. I'm going for a walk to go and buy something. I have money in my wallet."

Let me explain that this was Steven's first-ever sleepover at Grandma's house. He and Lucien, his 12-year-old brother, were in the guest bedroom, Steven on the queen bed and Lucien on the equally large air mattress. It was also after 10:00 pm.

"Steven, you are not going outside. You might get hit by a car, or someone could decide they wanted a little blonde boy and snatch you, and we'd never see you again.

"There's sidewalks so I won't get hit by a car. And I won't get stolen."

Steven's big brother yelled, "Go to sleep, Steven."

Like many kids, Steven hates to go to sleep at bedtime. His mom spends many nights reading book after book, rubbing his back, singing him songs, and begging him to please, please, please go to sleep.

My dog, the one that scares Steven a bit because he likes to jump up and say hi to everyone he sees, was on the air mattress, taking everything in.

With a big sigh, I implored this boy to sleep. We'd had a fun day of adding to his rock collection at the Rock and Gem show, followed by Sample Saturday at the Oshkosh Food Co-Op.

After that, a friend from my choral group had a party. Lucien and Steven enjoyed the other kids, there was an impressive buffet of pot-luck items, and, for dessert, s'mores. We left, averting a sugar-induced meltdown, and headed home to watch *Moana*.

It had been a wonderful day, but it was time for sleep. Nighttime talks with an intelligent and conversational little boy tend to bounce from topic to topic. But as riveting as those would be in the daytime, it was time to sleep.

"Steven, do you need to go to the bathroom?"

"Yes, Grandma." So we rolled off the big bed and walked down the hall to the bathroom.

"Grandma," he said as he rubbed his eyes. "I'm going to stay up all night. I'm not tired."

"I am," shouted his incredibly patient older brother. "Now go to sleep!"

"Do you need a drink of water, Steven?" When he nodded, I grabbed the cup of water on the nightstand, gave it to him, and watched him drain the cup.

I rubbed his back. Again. Told him a story. Again. And sang a song. Again. Then I came up with an idea.

"Can Coconut come and sleep next to you on the big bed? He's used to sleeping up here. I think he'd be happier. Is that okay?

He rubbed his eyes and nodded.

"Coconut, up!" Hearing the cue to go to his rightful place, Coconut scrambled from the air mattress to the bed in record time. He nestled in between the little boy who swore he would stay up all day and the exhausted grandma.

I looked over and saw a little hand begin to wave back and forth, back and forth over the dog. Coconut burrowed closer to Steven as the soothing touches continued. Steven's face relaxed and his eyes closed, leaving me to wonder why boys seem to have the longest, thickest eye lashes. And then it happened.

I heard Coconut's heavy sign of contentment at the exact time a breeze of sound exited Steven's mouth in a tiny puff.

Just like that, the little boy who was not going to sleep, who thought walking by himself to go shopping in the middle of the night was a smart idea, and who had resisted every trick I had tried, was hugging my dog, making little puffing sounds, and having little boy dreams.

A dog's unconditional love often reduces cortisol levels in children, which are associated with relaxation and stress reduction. The relaxing effect of interacting with a pup appears to be at least partially due to physical touch, so snuggling with Coconut eased Steven's mind and helped him to feel safe and tranquil.

Many times I've wished I lived back home in the land of sun and no snow. I loved my life back there. But that night wasn't one of those times. Curled up with my dog and Steven was exactly where I needed to be.

"Grandma, Grandma! I stayed up all night," Steven bragged the next morning.

"No you didn't, Steven," yelled his brother. "I heard you snoring."

I wisely kept quiet as the brothers bickered lightly amongst themselves. For the record, when I was awake, neither one of them snored. Nor did Coconut.

THE BEST OF THEM ALL
Margaret (Peg) Olson

"Dogs are our link to paradise."
— Milan Kundera

In 2017, my friend Kelly was fostering a dog named Jack, one of a group of dogs rescued from a puppy mill by the Wisconsin Westie Rescue. She wanted me to give him a forever home, but he was already seven years old. Three years earlier, I had lost Mac, my fourteen-year-old Westie, and I wasn't sure I was ready for a new dog.

"Just come and meet him. He'd make the perfect therapy dog," insisted Kelly.

She knew just what buttons to push because though I was retired, I had worked in the loss and grief field and remained interested in grief counseling. Once I met him, I agreed to adopt a senior dog.

The first thing I did was to rename him Alfie. It reminded me of the song made famous by the incomparable Dionne Warwick, and I sang it to him every day. The song implores us to give and to be kind, two things that come naturally to dogs.

With only three teeth, his diet was limited to soft food. The two cysts on Alfie's back didn't seem to bother him, and his typical westie allergies responded to medication.

Alfie was shy at first, but he soon met Jackson, who was owned by our backyard neighbor, the westie across the street, a German shepherd/mix, and Burley, the terrier who became our walking buddy.

Before long, Alfie became the hit of the neighborhood. He was welcome in anyone's home, he interacted with the people we met on our daily walks, and sat patiently and listened to one of the neighborhood children read books to him. Another child noticed that Alfie's tongue usually hung out because of his missing teeth. He said, "Alfie looks like he's thinking! It's like he has an idea!"

The best thing about Alfie was that he was intuitive. He always seemed to know who needed comfort. His kindness and calm, gentle nature made him a natural with hurting people.

I enjoyed countless instances of my puppy-mill-rescue making a difference in the lives of those he encountered. Some were friends, like the one we visited who cried while sharing about her dying daughter and others who were strangers.

One day while we were on our walk, we met a couple we knew just a little. We chatted for a few minutes only to have the woman sit on the sidewalk next to Alfie. Soon, she stood, smiled, and said, "I feel better now." I didn't know until later that she recently had been diagnosed with a serious health condition.

Being retired allowed me to volunteer with a local hospice program, and I often visited with patients at senior living communities. One such visit opened the door to exploring living options there when my husband's emphysema worsened. Moving turned out to be the perfect choice for us. Alfie might not have been in his old neighborhood, but he quickly became a favorite of everyone he met.

One of the nurses watched him interact politely with a very large dog visiting the resident in the next room. She suggested that he participate in their dog-training program. Alfie was a quick study and learned to climb the wheel of a wheelchair to make it easier for residents to pet him.

Once he completed his training, Alfie wasn't required to be on a leash, and the staff didn't fuss when he walked into the dining area. In fact, one day I found him patiently waiting while a staff member made a sandwich for him. Some residents kept dog treats in their rooms and spoiled him. Still another woman loved to pet Alfie, and he would stay with her until she fell asleep.

For all of his sweetness, my pooch was mischievous. He shoplifted toys at pet stores and once took one away from a little girl. Her grandparents bought her a new toy and wouldn't let me pay for it.

One of my favorite photos is of Alfie and two golden/white retrievers on the annual pet-blessing day at church. It was raining, and the usual outdoor service was held inside. When all the dogs, cats, and guinea pigs had received their blessings, Alfie noticed the retrievers' owner getting ready to hand out treats when they sat up nicely. Alfie quickly lined up next to the big dogs, sat up, and also received a treat.

As with any breed, westies are prone to certain medical conditions including allergies, digestive, skin, and dental problems. Our veterinarian helped us care for Alfie with knowledge, grace, and love throughout the challenges.

Alfie left us on a Saturday in May exactly as the noon siren wailed. I'd hoped for a few more years with this special dog because Alfie was such an intuitive and interesting dog as well as being my best buddy. I've had four wonderful dogs, but Alfie was exceptional. He was polite and friendly with people and most of the dogs we met on walks. Not only was he my best buddy, Alfie spread happiness to everyone he met. After a year and a half, I still envy the dog walkers I see every day.

When Alfie's condition worsened, he had having trouble walking up his ramp from the deck to the back door. He'd look up at me; I'd pick him up and set him on the top step. When he couldn't even get up on the deck, he'd walk around it and step up on the bricks around a small flower plot.

After Alfie died, the animal hospital sent a sympathy card with notes from the doctors and a packet of flower seeds. I planted the gift packet of seeds in that small area and added zinnia seeds this year. I wish I'd taken a picture of Alfie using his shortcut, but each year when new flowers bloom from seeds planted in his memory, I'll remember Alfie, the best of them all, on the bricks next to the flowers.

THE GIFT THAT RESCUED US ALL
Pat Severin

"Dogs and angels are not very far apart."
— Charles Bukowski

When my eighty-six-year-old mother adopted an American Eskimo/ cocker spaniel/mix, I was extremely upset. At this point in her life, she was widowed, lived alone, and needed a companion. The last ten years of her marriage she had cared for my father after a debilitating stroke until my father died. I understood her desire to not be alone after sixty-five years with my father, but a dog?

Mom was determined to get a dog despite some of her health issues that came with age. She didn't walk easily by herself. How could she care for a dog, feed him, take him to a vet, or out for a walk? I found myself imagining the worse. What if she tripped on his leash and broke her hip? She'd already broken both wrists a week apart. I failed to see how this was a good idea.

A couple had rescued a dog but soon found out that they could not give him the time he deserved. They placed an ad in the local newspaper, and Mom decided that was her dog.

Harley was a gorgeous, eye-catching white pup with light tan ears and spots. The stunning, plume-like tail was a tip of the hat to his cocker spaniel DNA. He was a medium dog and we had no other information about how he'd been treated, if he was trained, or if he was a good fit for Mom.

When I met Harley, he made me forget her age and any possible pitfalls. He was such a special soul and he and Mom bonded immediately. Everyone in the family felt it. Harley became one of the most exceptional dogs I'd ever known, and he couldn't have been a more appropriate gift for Mom. Gone were the misgivings and doubts; he was so much more than anyone could have expected.

It was beautiful to witness the special connection between my mother and Harley. He was more than a dog, more than a companion. He had a sixth sense about her and, in his own way, did his best to care for her. If she dropped something, he'd get it rather than have her stoop down. He was always right there, her shadow, always at her side.

Earlier I mentioned that my mother had fallen and broken both wrists a week apart. I was afraid she'd break a hip, and unfortunately, that's what happened. But Harley was not to blame. She missed the kitchen chair and landed on the floor and had to be taken to the hospital by ambulance. We all were worried sick, and so was Harley.

When the entire family had a short meeting with the doctor, he pointed out a few things that discouraged us. Mom was less than the perfect surgical candidate. She was almost eighty-nine, frail, and had emphysema from a lifetime of smoking. All these factors made the outcome anything but a good bet. The doctor was kind but honest, as he told us to be prepared if she didn't make it through surgery.

None of us would have been surprised if she hadn't made it, but she did survive. We knew that she would have to go to a facility for rehab, and that meant months away from us and her beloved Harley. The rehab facility was in a nursing home, which she dreaded because she felt that once you go to a place like that you'll never come home.

One of us had to care for Harley in her absence, and that pleasure fell to my husband and me. That poor dog missed my mother terribly, but for Mom, getting home to her Harley was just the incentive she needed to work hard on her therapy. She did make it home in a few months, wheelchair and all, and the two of them reunited.

The joyful reunion was short-lived, and nine days later, a week before her eighty-ninth birthday, Mom fell victim to an unrelenting neck pain. She was given a dose of pain medication that finally gave her relief. However, it also caused her to go into a coma and pass away.

Dearest Harley became ours permanently, but only for a few years. One evening he had what the vet felt was a stroke of sorts. After that, he couldn't recognize anyone and stopped eating. One by one the family came to say their final goodbyes, and Harley was euthanized.

That was, indeed, a terrible day for all of us, but we were thankful for the time we had. Although he was a rescue, the truth is, Harley was the gift that rescued us all.

LIFE AFTER GOODBYE
Melinda Schmidt

"Pets are humanizing. They remind us we have an obligation and responsibility to preserve and nurture and care for all life."
— James Cromwell

After losing several dogs as a child, my tender-hearted husband couldn't imagine getting close to another dog that would eventually pass away. We met, married, raised two children, and that, or so I thought, was that.

Life without a dog was fine with Dave, but everything changed when our daughter's friend needed a home for Pippa, a long-haired Chihuahua/miniature pinscher/mix puppy. Pippa was the four-month-old runt of the litter, whom everyone said looked like a fox

I could brush off the comparison until a policeman stopped to admire our darling new baby. "It, well, it looks like a fox," declared the officer. I quickly laughed and went on my way before he asked any questions.

Dave was in love with our Pip from the start and, like everyone else with a dog, he thought she was the greatest pooch in the world. For some reason I can no longer remember, he came to call her the $94,000 show dog. To him, she was priceless.

Soon he would do anything and everything for Pip. I used to tease him that he would question one of my insignificant purchases, but when I announced how much a vet or grooming appointment had cost, he'd shrug it off, because nothing was too good for his $94,000 show dog.

I had heard Chihuahuas can live to about nineteen years old, so I filed that away and assumed we had many years ahead with her. We looked forward to having Pip grow old with us, though I guess in the eyes of our kids, we were already old.

Pip had a significant heart murmur, digestive issues, and occasional seizures, but we were captivated by this dog, and that was as far as we could see! Our eight-pound girl was a snuggler, loyal, loved going everywhere with us and was glued to us every minute of every day. We gave her lots of nicknames, babied her, and welcomed each day with her in our home.

Soon after turning eleven, she developed a cough that sounded suspiciously like a cat with a hairball. We were moving, and a trip to a new vet meant x-rays and eventually waiting for the health crisis the doctor predicted would come with her newly diagnosed, congestive heart failure.

That crisis came sooner than we expected, and very quickly we faced the decision of whether or not to end her suffering brought on her lack of appetite and increased difficulty breathing. Five days after we moved into our home in a new town, we said goodnight and goodbye to our Pip. On that dark, damp, and cold Sunday night, in an unfortunately equally dark and emotionally cold emergency vet clinic, we let her go. We were not prepared for that experience.

We began the unwelcome navigation of shock over losing Pip so quickly and grieving that she wouldn't be a part of our new-home life with us. As I posted about Pip on Facebook, people told their own stories of pet loss and gave us virtual hugs and understanding.

As the weeks went on, we noticed that as we appreciated the willing listeners, cards, texts and even remembrance gifts, we were much more aware of some others' grief. We became more sensitive to the struggles of those in our own circle and even unseen faces around the world. Our heartbreak lengthened and strengthened our empathy muscle, and we developed a stronger connection to people we knew and people we didn't know. We thought our hearts were full with Pip in our lives, but in her passing, our hearts were beginning to expand more, even giving us a new compassion for our very planet.

We became more attuned to others who were shocked and grief-stricken by their own kinds of losses: the loss of a spouse, a beloved pet, a job, a lost client, the loss of a dream, a disappointment, a divorce, a new diagnosis, a catastrophic weather event, a move, or another life change. We became more aware of opportunities to send a card, a long-distance food delivery, flowers, or plant a tree in someone's memory.

We increased our charitable giving for our community and other national and global needs. In the first months, we gave monetary gifts to pet rescues or other non-profits in Pip's honor. These ways of giving helped us to mourn and honor the delightful years we'd had with her.

Slowly, as we felt our grief, we attended a pet-loss support group and connected with others who were willing to engage with our journey. Our difficult experience of losing Pip served to grow us into better human beings. Pip might no longer be with us, but we could continue to honor the blessing of her life by extending care to others.

And interestingly, our marriage shifted to include more compassion for each other. Losing Pip was just about the worst thing that could ever happen, and we found we inadvertently quit fussing with each other about things that, although significant in a new move, now invited us to be gentle with each other, treating each other with new respect. Compared to losing Pip, some things were no longer as important or worth so much fretting. We practiced more love and enjoyment in our marriage, and we listened and loved each other better.

Going the distance this year after the loss of the greatest dog in the world has meant practicing strength, learning how to do this kind of grief, and developing more empathy for others' losses. We've worked at developing our creativity when reaching out and honoring others' grief in meaningful ways. We know what the comfort of others—even some we will never meet in person—has meant to us. They took time to acknowledge our grief when we were too tired, too hurt, or too embarrassed, as we managed the surprising bigness of it.

Our lives are now bittersweet, a mix of fun and loving memories of Pip whose presence we continue to miss, while we also cherish and appreciate the ways knowing her—and now losing her—have enriched our lives and subsequently, others' lives.

WHAT DO YOU SEE?
Marsha Hubler

"My shelter days are over, done, because you,
my master, took me home."
— Courtney Bailey

At 3:15 on a terrible morning last year, Marsha's sweet Bailey, whom she adopted from the SPCA thirteen years ago, crossed over the Rainbow Bridge.

An area farmer brought his posthole digger to fashion the hole that would later hold the remains of Marsha's beloved dog. They buried Bailey under the pines out back. It was a rough day, one that will take time to settle into. There's always a special pet everyone has. Bailey was that one to her.

A while back, Marsha wrote a poem dedicated to all rescue dogs. When she shared on Facebook about the loss of Bailey, I reached out to her, and she graciously gave me permission to share this poem with you.

This is a tribute to a very special dog in her life, one who gave her the greatest joy any fur-kid could ever have done for the last thirteen years.

As you read these words think of your special dog, the one whom you rescued who in turn rescued you.

(Dedicated to all dogs who've found their forever homes and are now loved more than they've been hurt.)

WHAT DO YOU SEE?
　　What do you see when you stare up at me?
　　Soon to be kicked out in the dark city?
　　Does your past life force you to run and hide?

Or does my smile say to come by my side?
I see stares of fear but then gleams of hope
To never be tied with a chain or a rope;
You won't be bitten by ticks and bad bugs;
I'll always feed you and give you warm hugs.

So, I wonder . . .

What do you see when you stare up at me?
Will you run away if I let you go free?
Please look deep into my eyes and my smile;
I'll love you forever, not for a while.

LATCHING THE GARDEN GATE
HOSTAS
WELCOME

WELCOME HOME

"A garden is a grand teacher. It teaches patience
and careful watchfulness; it teaches industry and thrift;
above all it teaches entire trust."
— Gertrude Jekyll

A few years ago, as the gardening season was winding down, I needed to move a bunch of Hostas. The Latin roots of the name "hosta" suggest a sense of hospitality and welcome. They loved the sun and offered a warm welcome flanking each side of the driveway. But they grew into big, floppy, and ultimately sloppy Hostas, making them a target for every tire. The smashed plants annoyed me, and I knew I needed to move them, but by that time, I was sick of gardening.

I posted on the Facebook Wisconsin Gardening Group wondering if someone would come and help me move plants because my husband was recovering from a hip replacement. I didn't expect anyone to actually respond, except to tell me to quit my whining and get to work. That's not how the story ends.

Her name is Sandy, and she lives in my town. Much to my delight, Sandy said she'd be happy to come and help me move those plants. Sure enough, she came with some gardening tools and gloves. Sandy is an outstanding gardener. I am not. Sandy bakes sourdough bread from starter. I don't do that either. She grows food, makes jam, knits, and is an overachiever in every way. Instead of gardening, we sat inside the house sharing stories and becoming friends.

Sandy didn't pull out plants that day, so I jokingly call her the gardener who doesn't garden. But she did give my dog lots of attention, and that was another connection that has made our friendship grow.

Hostas are super easy to grow and they are a welcome addition to any garden as long as you know the sunlight requirements. My first Hostas were given to me by a friend and I plunked them down in a recently cleared area. It didn't take too long to realize that these rescue Hostas were shade plants. I added different varieties but by July they were burned and distressed.

When my kids were little we had a dog named Brutus. He was an oops puppy because his owners had not gotten their dog spayed. What I learned from Brutus is that goldendoodles are high energy, they need lots of room, separation anxiety is a real thing, and, if not trained and exercised, all sorts of bad things will happen to everything you own.

Brutus was adorable and free and the absolutely wrong animal for our tiny house with two working adults and an unfenced yard. Kind of like my Hostas during those first few years that we planted them in full sun. The good news is that someone with nine acres in the country fell in love with Brutus and he went to live with her and grew into the dog he was always meant to be.

Just as there are many varieties of Hostas there are an immense number of dog breeds and breed mixes but not every dog is a good fit for every family or home. And not every plant will thrive in every garden. Don't worry, I was able to find homes for all of those Hostas. They are one of the easiest plants to split and rehome so I invited people to come and take these hearty and welcoming plants to their gardens and I replaced them with other flora that can handle the sun.

When I adopted Coconut, I knew absolutely nothing about the world of animal rescue. Now I've learned that most rescues in my area are actually foster-to-adoption groups and are, for the most part, staffed with volunteers. This means more of the adoption costs and donations go to rescuing dogs instead of paying various costs associated with being in a brick-and-mortar business. A key component of many rescues is that they have with a network of foster families committed to helping the dogs.

The foster-to-adoption model of rescue allows volunteers to offer a dog a short-term welcome on their way to a long-term, and hopefully, forever home.

This ending section highlights ways that people have gotten involved in the rescue dog world. There's a piece from Sandy, the gardener who really does garden who also happens to be a foster mom, and an introduction to Second Chance Shelter in Boaz, Alabama and Second Chance North in Northeast Wisconsin. The final story is from a volunteer extraordinaire who helps dogs and other animals in a variety of ways.

A latched garden gate symbolizes a place of safety, which is what both our plants and dogs need. The hospitality and welcome that volunteers offer in both models is why thousands of dogs a year have safe and loving, forever homes.

ONE DOG AT A TIME

Sandra Dennis

"It's a small thing to help one animal,
but to that one animal it's a big thing."
— Gene Baur.

My husband and I showed our Dalmatians, and that meant being around all types of breeds. All dogs have something special about them, but I always admired the gentle nature of the cavalier king Charles spaniels I saw at dog shows and our kennel club. All those I knew were smart and loving. A fellow Dalmatian exhibitor also had cavaliers. She called them her "old lady dogs." Since I recently retired and am now a widow, a cavalier seemed like the breed for me.

I started by adopting Sadie, a seven-year-old breeder surrender, through the Cavalier Rescue Midwest in 2020. She had been a puppy mama her entire life. We are best friends and she taught me many things—how to be patient and brave when things are scary, how to snuggle really close to your best friend, even if it means creating a tiny amount of space next to your human in the chair.

After a year or so, we started fostering other dogs.

Many dogs that come into the rescue are commercial breeder surrenders, meaning they most likely have spent their entire lives in a breeding barn with little human interaction. Many of them are viewed as livestock. Some were given to the rescue because they were no longer viable for breeding.

At times, whole litters of ill-bred puppies are turned over to the rescue due to health concerns or defects the breeder didn't want to deal with. Cavaliers are prone to certain eye, heart, and joint issues.

In all cases, the dogs need socialization and the opportunity to learn how to be a dog.

Dogs in the rescue are put on a nutrient-dense raw diet to restore them to a healthy state. Thorough health exams are done to identify issues, all are brought up to date on vaccinations, spayed or neutered, and given much-needed health care. It's not unusual for dental issues to be extensive for dogs coming into the rescue —dental care is practically non-existent with commercial breeders. Health issues that can be fixed or stabilized are taken care of. Even when a rescue team partners with generous veterinarians, the costs of getting some dogs into an adoptable health condition is far greater than any adoption fee will cover.

Coming into a rescue is a giant mental adjustment for the dogs, too. That's where foster homes come in. A foster home introduces them to "the good life."

Some of the dogs are so scared; some fear humans. Everything is new to them—sounds of a television, door bells, vacuum cleaners, normal sounds within a home.

Many have never experienced things like stairs, stepping on grass, or going for walks on a leash. Potty training is always a work in progress. Some learn quickly, while others take a while for the light to go on. I'm thankful for hard floors. My little area rug has almost been completely cleaned, one spot at a time. My house has been puppy-proofed because they all start out that way, regardless of age.

Most dogs figure out life with humans. Unfortunately, some remain too scared or withdrawn or have serious health issues that make them unadoptable. These few become forever fosters who stay in foster care their entire lives, where they receive the ongoing love and support that they deserve.

As a foster home, Sadie and I welcome new dogs, and they stay with us until a match is made, linking them to their forever home. Just like children, they come with their own set of fears and idiosyncrasies.

Our first foster was Toby—a six-year-old boy that came from a commercial breeder. He was infested with fleas, and his skin was in terrible shape. Over time, his coat grew back, and it was beautiful. We had him for a couple of months. Toby learned that toys, especially those with squeakers, were great things. He loved paper of any kind—turning boxes into confetti was his thing. Toby never jumped up, but would look longingly at you with his big brown eyes and was thrilled when you lifted him into your lap. Toby's forever home is in Michigan.

Next there was Bonnie, a two-year-old who wasn't cut out to be a puppy mama and was surrendered by a commercial breeder. She was the closest to coming to us as a real dog of those we've fostered. House breaking took a while, especially when it was snowy outside. She loved everyone and everything and was quick to jump into the laps of visitors and give middle-of-the-night kisses when you rolled over in bed. I believe the fact that she was only in a commercial breeding operation for a couple of years led to her resilience. Yet, Bonnie had her quirks, too – like alerting you to when the neighbors were out next door. When a puppy barked on the television there was no stopping Bonnie from adding her voice to the chorus. She's an expert mid-air popcorn catcher, loves walks, and found a great home in Chicago, where she supervises her work-from-home mom and has made lots of dog and people friends.

Tomorrow, we get Jimmy. He's a three-year-old breeder surrender that I'm told is a little shy and working on house training. Our intake home says he's a little goofy. Bring it on, Jimmy—we like goofy. That means you're learning to relax and trust. You're well on your way to being a real dog and enjoying the good life!

FIND A NEED

"People become really quite remarkable when they start thinking that they can do things. When they believe in themselves, they have the first secret of success."
— Norman Vincent Peale

In 1968, Norman Vincent Peale, American Protestant clergyman, author, and co-founder of Guideposts Magazine, said that "find a need and fill it" was his six-word formula for success. That premise is true for both for-profit and non-profit companies world-wide.

That's exactly what Doug and Wanda McGee did when they started rescuing dogs. The need that they saw couldn't wait for business plans and getting their non-profit tax status. The situation presented itself, and they acted on impulse—and they were off to the races.

As Doug says, "I was working as a police officer at the Albertville, Alabama Police Department. One day in May of 2008, the dispatcher was on the phone, so when the other line rang, I answered it. The caller asked if we would send animal control to his house because someone had just dropped off seven puppies."

Being a 19-year veteran, Doug knew animal control worked under the umbrella of the police department so he was familiar with their protocol. He realized if animal control got the puppies, they would be destroyed that day.

He hung up and instantly called Wanda and said, "Some puppies are going to die today if we don't get them. Can we bring them to the house and find them homes?"

Without hesitation she agreed, and he went to the house in his patrol car and picked up the puppies and put them in the caged back seat. By the time he got home, they had made an incredibly smelly mess, but that was okay.

At that time, the City of Albertville was euthanizing around 130 stray, abandoned, or unwanted dogs a month. Let that sink in. If we do the math that's 1,560 helpless animals killed every year.

Doug and Wanda cared for those babies until they all found loving homes, and Second Chance Shelter of Boaz began to take shape. There was no grand plan, no financial preparedness, and not much foresight at all. Their only real thought on that fateful day was to save the lives of those seven puppies.

Like every rescue and shelter, they are underfunded and survive on donations, the occasional grant, and, as is the case of Jerry, the kindness of strangers. Jerry had moved back to Boaz, Alabama from Panama City Beach, Florida to be closer to his aging parents in 2008.

He lived on a farm in an area that is a dumping ground for unwanted dogs. Jerry kept the first four dumped dogs, but after that, he started using Facebook to help find homes for the continuing stream of puppies and older dogs.

One day in the spring of 2012, Jerry walked out of his farm and found a little puppy standing on the floorboard of the golf cart staring at him. He picked her up, wondering where she came from and what to do. He decided to take her to his vet's office. They suggested he go to Second Chance Shelter to see if the shelter had room for her. He'd never heard of this shelter, even though he only lived about eight miles away.

When he arrived, the owner was at the gate, talking to a family. When the family left, Jerry asked Doug if he could take the puppy since he already had four rescue dogs and had no room for more.

Doug agreed, and Jerry gave him a donation and asked about the shelter. After learning more details, Jerry asked if Second Chance ever let people come in and volunteer.

Jerry's first day of volunteering involved cleaning the kennels, scrubbing water bowls, and filling those same bowls. As time went on, Jerry volunteered between three to seven days a week.

Jerry noticed that each kennel was identified by a sign on that kennel, such as A - 1. He offered to take pictures of each dog, edit and laminate the pictures, and affix them to the kennel. That was his first big project at the shelter. He also creates all of the collages/pictures, which helps get dogs adopted more quickly.

Jerry is a retired school principal and is devoted to the shelter's success. He never planned on being a volunteer at an animal shelter. But it's because of people like Jerry and other dedicated volunteers that Second Chance Shelter can continue to save lives each month.

One of the challenges of an independent shelter is finding homes for all of the dogs that continue to pour in. Wisconsin doesn't have a stray dog problem. In fact, it can be hard to find adoptable pups, so many groups bring dogs here from locations that have an over-abundance of rescues needing homes.

In 2018 Rebecca, Jessica, her husband, Jason, first met Wanda and the crew at Second Chance Shelter. At that time they were volunteers for a different rescue group in Wisconsin. After a few years, they left that organization but kept in touch with Wanda.

"We knew our journey in dog rescue wasn't finished," explains Rebecca. "We also knew we wanted to figure out a way to specifically help Doug and Wanda. After throwing around ideas and collaborating with our friend, Carrie, who works in the veterinary industry, Second Chance North, a foster-to-adoption rescue, was born."

Their first transport was in the fall of 2020 during the heart of a pandemic. Despite the timing, they continue to transport dogs up to Northeast Wisconsin where they find loving, forever families.

When Doug and Wanda rescued those first seven dogs, they didn't expect to open a shelter and quit their day jobs. Jerry probably had a different vision for how he would spend retirement. Rebecca, Jessica, Jason, and Carrie never envisioned themselves rescuing and rehoming dogs from Alabama to Wisconsin. These seven people, and countless volunteers and foster families, believed and achieved, and, along the way, saved lives and created families.

PAYING HOMAGE TO OUR DOGS
Cheryl Hentz

"All his life he tried to be a good person.
Many times, however, he failed.
For after all, he was only human. He wasn't a dog."
— Charles M. Schulz

I've been around dogs my entire life. We always had a dog growing up, and as an adult, I've never been without at least one dog.

Anyone who has had the honor, and responsibility, of owning a dog knows the unconditional love they give us; and the unconditional love that a true dog lover gives them. No matter how bad a day we, or they, may have had, they are there with snuggles, kisses, adoring eyes, and unbridled love to bestow upon us.

And yet, our dogs never live long enough. As the end draws near, we long for just one more day, one more kiss, one more snuggle.

But there's another lesson besides unconditional love that we can learn from a dog. And that is that, no matter what life throws at you, you must keep on going.

All the dogs I've ever had have come from rescues or shelters (or were on their way to ending up in one). Most have been perfectly healthy when we adopted them, but a couple had some minor physical challenges. The others, as they aged, developed one problem or another. A couple of them lost their hearing, and all of them became ill with cancer or some other life-altering illness.

Yet, they just kept plugging away. Some days may have been worse for them than others, but they always found a way to show their unwavering love; and they always found a way to keep persevering and live their lives to the fullest—no matter what!

That's not just a wonderful lesson about living life to the fullest; it's a laudable goal to shoot for.

Life is always bound to throw curve balls our way or put hurdles in our path. Those things help keep us on our toes and, believe it or not, can help keep life interesting. But when I think back to the beautiful, loving dogs I've had the pleasure of sharing my life with, I think about how they never let things keep them down.

Many years ago, I promised myself that no matter what happened in my life, I would honor the dogs I've had throughout my life. I would find a way to get "back on my feet" and keep pushing on when some life event knocked me down. I would have to keep on going, to love and care for the dogs I currently own, but to also pay homage to all those dogs I used to own and that are still watching over me and providing motivation and inspiration for me today.

CONTRIBUTORS

Stevie Anderson is a simple woman who loves puppies. She has a 13-year-old Pomeranian, Mario; a 12-year-old foster fail, Tay; a three-year-old Chihuahua, Lucy; and Joey, an 18-month-old foster fail.

Sally Apokedak lives in cozy home in the North Georgia mountains with her sweet pals and hiking buddies, Heidi the Pyrenees and Brandy the Dutch Shepherd. Learn more about Sally's boutique publishing press by visiting paraklesispressbooks.com.

Margo Bennet is a dedicated puppy raiser and author of the children's book series *Tails of Dogs Who Help*. All book proceeds are donated to schools where the dogs are trained. Margot is married with four children and lives in North Carolina. To learn more about her books visit dogswhohelp.com.

Charlotte H. Burkholder is a wife, grandmother, great-grandmother, and happy owner of 'Lil Daze. She is active in her local writer's group.

Janet Charbonneau is an IT Consultant who loves spending time with her golden retriever, Holly, and volunteering for dog and military-related non-profits. She enjoys taking the road less traveled and has written and published books about her adventures. Follow her at Facebook.com/JanetCharbonneauAuthor.

Zeta Combs Davidson's book, *Strength for the Sadness*, is available on Amazon. She may be reached at zetacombsdavidson.com or on Facebook. Zeta serves on the leadership team of Heart of America Christian Writers Network.

236 · WHEN LOVE WAGS A TAIL

Xochitl (So-Cheel) Dixon, *Our Daily Bread* writer and author of *Waiting for God, What Color is God's Love?* and *Different Like Me,* celebrates diversity and inclusion with her beautifully diverse family and her service dog, Callie. You can learn more at xedixon.com.

Eileen Joyce Donovan's historical novels, *Promises, A Lady Newspaperman's Dilemma,* and *The Campbell Sisters* have won national awards. Her short stories have appeared in assorted themed anthologies and her non-fiction essays in various editions of Chicken Soup for the Soul. Visit her at ejdonovan.com.

Carolyn Fisher became a serious writer after becoming a widow. She writes poetry for requested events, such as birthdays, anniversaries, etc. She can be reached at carolyn.fisher61@gmail.com

Peggy Frezon is contributing editor of *Guideposts* and *Angels on Earth* magazines, and author of books about the human-animal bond. She rescues senior golden retrievers. Find out about her books, and sign up for her newsletter, Dogs of BrooksHaven, at peggyfrezon.com. Follow her on Facebook.com/PeggyFrezonBooks.

Michele Miles Gardiner enjoys storytelling and finding the humor in life's chaos—as she does in *Craving Normal* and her upcoming book, *How to Stay Broke and Influence Nobody.* To learn more about her book, visit michelemilesgardiner.com.

Mary J. Hahn is a tall, gorgeous, blond, and very married, mom, and grandmom. Mary is a former IT project manager, active in the League of Women Voters, a WINGS volunteer, a certified TreeKeeper, and is learning to play the piano for fun.

Gerald Hendrickson is a chiropractor, a member of the Oshkosh Rotary Southwest, a husband, dad to two sons, and granddad to Dylan,

Jaxon, William, and Claire. He's also a dog dad, a fact that should have possibly gotten top billing.

Cheryl D. Hentz is a freelance journalist/talk show host with forty-plus years in print and broadcast journalism. When not working, she enjoys spending time with her dog(s), pet-sitting for others, and volunteering with dog rescue groups, shelters, and animal welfare organizations. Learn more about Cheryl at Cherylhentz.blogspot.com.

Marsha Hubler is the author of the best-selling Keystone Stables Series. She has a master's degree in education and fifty-plus years working with children. Besides owning horses, she's loved two dogs at a time for most of her adult life, the majority rescued canines. Visit her at marshahublerauthor.com.

In 2017, after a career in politics, **Don Hughes** found his true calling while volunteering at the Maricopa County Animal Care and Control West Shelter as an adoption counselor. In 2018, he helped 275 dogs and eighteen cats find forever homes. Learn more about Don at donhughesauthor.com.

Andrea Hunter is a writer currently situated on her wanna-be homestead in the suburbs of Chicago. Her work has appeared in *Wingless Dreamer's Wild Heart, Up the Staircase Quarterly, Fauxmoir Literary Magazine, Sad Girl Diaries, Shady Grove Literary,* and more. Learn more about Andrea at andreahunterwrites.com and follow her on Instagram at@andrea.hunter3.

Andie LaComb is a dog lover and rescue volunteer. She loves hiking and kayaking with her dogs and husband. Her first book, *Adventures with Karli*e, chronicles her adventures with her senior rescue dog in California and Indiana. Learn more about Andie by visiting LiveLikeKarlie.com.

Brenda Kay Ledford is a retired educator and professional writer. Her work has appeared in many journals. Her latest book, *Leatherwood Falls: Blue Ridge Mountain Poems,* received the 2023 Award of Excellence from North Carolina Society of Historians. She blogs at blueridgepoet.blogspot.com

Kristine Lowder is a professional book reviewer and multi-published author. She has a degree in communication/print media from Biola University. She thinks everything is better with a dog. (Except maybe cookies 'n' cream ice cream.) Enjoy her reviews and more at pagesandpaws.com.

Susan E. Mullaney is a retired marketing and communications professional who now devotes her energy to rescuing and rehoming Australian Shepherds for Australian Shepherds Furever, a national non-profit. She and husband, Don, live at Maple Shade Farm with their five Aussies, horses, alpacas and chickens. Her website is MapleShadeFarmME.com.

Rosie Maureen has been a salesperson, poet, advocate for children, and a mother of two. She and her husband share their home in Southern California with two extraordinarily rescued pets (Jubilee Joy and Wondrous Joy) and a lifetime collection of books.

Leola R. Ogle lives in Arizona with her husband, Jeff, and their two rescue dogs. They have a large blended family of eight children, many grandchildren, and great-grandchildren. Leola has authored several novels plus several published short stories. She and her husband have been in ministry most of their adult lives. Her passion is to write about real life issues based on her ministry and family experiences.

Margaret (Peg) Olson is a retired school counselor/university counselor educator who has lived with dogs most of her life. Her newest buddy is Lucy, a small five-year-old rescue poodle.

Janet Pfeiffer, international speaker, radio host, holistic life coach, and award-winning author, provides workshops on interpersonal skills to Fortune 500 companies. She also speaks on spirituality at retreats. Her books include *The Secret Side of Anger* and *The Great Truth.* For more information visit PfeifferPowerSeminars.com.

Diane Huff Pitts is a rescue dog lover and is currently ruled by the two cats who chose her family. Living in a rural Gulf Coast community with her husband, Darrell, she writes about God connections in family, health, and the world about us. Visit Diane at dianehuffpitts.com.

Anne Rauth and her family—husband Scott and their three sons, Benjamin, Jameson and 'Topher—have rescued three dogs: Bailey, Abbie the Labbie, and Holly the Collie. Anne would love to connect with you at annerauth.com and at Facebook.com/AnneRauthAuthor.

Elizabeth Ritzman is an ordained minister, a therapist, retired college health center director, and dog mom of two. Learn more about her at elizabethritzman.com.

Roxanne Rolph has owned dogs most of her adult life. She and husband, Fred, have been married thirty-three years, have two children and two grandchildren. Roxanne enjoys spending time with family and doing crafts with her grandchildren.

Melinda Schmidt's life evolved into a decades-long career in national radio. After her and Dave's kids left home, she and Dave got a dog, the caramel-colored, long-haired chi/min pin Pippa, who looked like a fox, and they loved her forever, even after she left them. Visit her website at tidescoaching.co and follow her on Facebook at facebook.com/melinda.schmidt.

Pat Severin is a seasoned writer who has been penning poems and essays for years. She is published in many magazines as well as *Chicken Soup for the Soul* and her story was featured in *I Chose You, Imperfectly Perfect Rescue Dogs and Their Humans*. Pat has two children and three grandchildren.

Ellie Ray Spivey taught kindergarten thirty-one years. She now enjoys kayaking, taking Tai-Chi classes, butterfly gardening, and snuggling with her rescue dog, Gus. Ellie Ray is also a founder of a local group called "Dolls on a Mission."

Tricia Stertz is a midwestern gal, minister's wife, retired critical care nurse, and a new great grandmother. She is a lover of travel, reading, writing, beauty of all kinds, and, most of all, a lover of people.

Carla Stewart is the award-winning author of six novels and numerous magazine articles. She and her husband live in Texas and enjoy weekend getaways, the busy lives of their grandchildren, and chasing after Penny PopTart, their rescue pup. Learn more at carlastewart.com.

Janice Thompson is a Christian author from Spring, Texas. She is passionate about her faith, her family, and baking. She's also over-the-moon for dogs, which is why she writes so many of them into her tails (er, *tales*). When she's not busy writing, you'll find Janice in the kitchen baking treats for humans . . . and canines! Learn more about Janice by visiting janiceathompson.com and follow her at Facebook.com/JaniceHannaThompson.

Christine Trollinger is a writer, mother, and widow who has been a writer for over twenty years. She has written for *Guideposts, Chicken Soup for The Soul, God allows U-Turns, Ascension Press, Kansas City Star,* and many more.

Gail Westrup is a retired journalist who loves dogs and really loves Golden Retrievers. She and her husband, Doug, live in Northern California, and when they aren't traveling with their dog Merry, they volunteer at Homeward Bound Golden Retriever Rescue.

Born in Canada, **Quentin Wood** moved to Wisconsin over 20 years ago. He strives to walk the middle path while enjoying yoga, meditation, sharing his love of dogs, and, above all, being a father. Learn more about Quentin at bodhibowwow.com.

ACKNOWLEDGEMENTS

One day last year I happened to see a Facebook post about a pet photography event featuring Aaron Jankowski, an Oshkosh-based photographer who specializes in pet portraiture. We went and Aaron did a terrific job of getting some fun photos of Coconut that evening.

When I decided I wanted few photos of Coconut and me together for my author photo, despite not liking to be held, and after many, many dog treats, Aaron managed to get a shot that didn't look like Coconut is in a hostage situation.

Creating a cover is always a challenge. I looked at dozens of photos and finally realized that Aaron would probably have the perfect dog. Thank you, Aaron, for your love of dogs and your willingness to let me showcase your remarkable work. I'll forgive you for not shaving off the promised thirty extra pounds of baby weight I've been holding on to for forty-two years. You can follow Aaron and a.pet.ture and book a photography session at facebook.com/aaron.jankowski.

Now that you have come to the end of this book, you know I am not the best-natured gardener out there. Thank you to the Wisconsin Gardening Group for being supportive and helpful as we tamed this yard of ours. Special thanks to the Oshkosh Garden Club for trusting us with one of the six coveted slots on the 2023 Oshkosh Garden Walk.

I would be remiss if I did not mention the Oshkosh businesses that welcomed me with open arms when it came time for book signings. If you are in Fox Valley, do yourself a favor and check out the following people and their wonderful businesses: Sandi Zeibell of Fabulous Finds, Steve Aherns of Firehouse Subs, Melissa and Sonia and Ochowicz of The Turquoise Door Oshkosh, and Brian Pribbernow of uBloom Floral Design.

Thank you to everyone who bought a copy of *I Chose You, Imperfectly Perfect Rescue Dogs and Their Humans*. Thanks to you

I've been able to donate money to Second Chance Shelter of Boaz, Alabama and Second Chance North here in Northeast Wisconsin. To learn more about this amazing rescue or to make a donation, go to secondchanceshelter.biz.

Thank you to everyone who shared their dog's story this time around and to Cheri Cowell of EABooks Publishing, my meticulous and fabulous editor, Jeanette Gardner Littleton, my amazingly talented cover designer, Robin Black, and my author liaison, Rebecca Ford.

I could and probably should name more people who helped me to get this manuscript ready for publication. I hate missing anyone so I am going to limit myself to one special friend.

When I was in high school, Carol Vogel was on the selection committee and chose me to be a foreign exchange student from Topeka, Kansas to Sao Paulo, Brazil with the AFS program. I can never say thank you enough to her for playing such a huge role in my life. We are Facebook friends and I asked her if she would like an advance copy of the manuscript to review. She not only said yes, but did a marvelous job of proofreading without being asked. This was a gift I can never repay as I had eye surgery in August of 2023 and this March and detail work is still difficult. Being friends with a former college professor came in handy!

The last thanks goes to my husband for being my chauffeur when I could not drive and for creating my websites and all the wonderful marketing graphics. I could never do them on my own.

244 • WHEN LOVE WAGS A TAIL

PHOTO CREDITS

Opening the Garden Gate   Nathalie Spehner

Chapter One   Nathalie Spehner

Chapter Two   Duncan Sanchez

Chapter Three   Jonny Neuenhagen

Chapter Four   Jairo Alzate

Chapter Five   Ralu Gal

Chapter Six   Karsten Winegeart

Chapter Seven   Jay Wennington

Chapter Eight   Abigail Baines

Latching the Garden Gate   Courtney Mihaka

Dear Reader,

Thank you for loving rescue dogs and for allowing me to share these stories with you. There truly are not enough words to express how much your support means to Coconut and me.

If you enjoyed my book, I would appreciate if you would scan the QR code below to leave a review. Your feedback in incredibly valuable to me and it helps other readers discover my book.

Thank you so much for being a part of my journey. Aloha

Carmen

www.ingramcontent.com/pod-product-compliance
Lightning Source LLC
Chambersburg PA
CBHW030822090426
42737CB00009B/835